Poetry as Prayer
Emily Dickinson

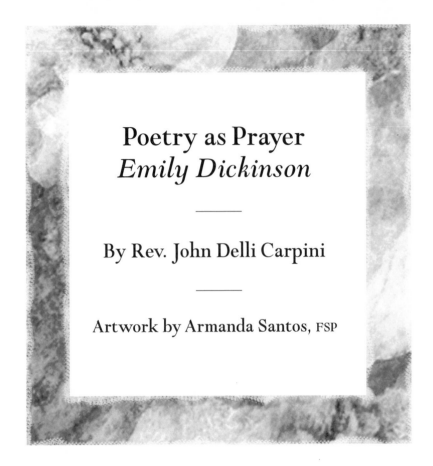

Poetry as Prayer
Emily Dickinson

———

By Rev. John Delli Carpini

———

Artwork by Armanda Santos, FSP

Pauline
BOOKS & MEDIA
BOSTON

Library of Congress Cataloging-in-Publication Data

Delli Carpini, John

   Poetry as prayer: Emily Dickinson / by John Delli Carpini ; artwork by Armanda Santos, FSP.

      p. cm. (The poetry as prayer series)

   Includes bibliographical references.

   ISBN 0-8198-5935-4 (pbk.)

      1. Dickinson, Emily, 1830–1886 Criticism and interpretation. 2. Religious poetry, American History and criticism. 3. Dickinson, Emily, 1830–1886 Religion. 4. Prayer in literature.

   I. Title. II. Series.

PS1541.Z5 D45 2002

811'.4   dc21

                           2001007979

Poems in this volume reprinted by permission of the publishers and the Trustees of Amherst College from THE POEMS OF EMILY DICKINSON, Thomas H. Johnson, ed., Cambridge, MA: The Belknap Press of Harvard University Press, Copyright © 1951, 1955, 1979 by the President and Fellows of Harvard College.

Letters quoted in this volume reprinted by permission of the publishers from THE LETTERS OF EMILY DICKINSON, edited by Thomas H. Johnson, Cambridge, MA: The Belknap Press of Harvard University Press, Copyright © 1958, 1986 by the President and Fellows of Harvard College.

The author has donated royalty proceeds from sales of this title to the Missionary Sisters of the Sacred Heart of Jesus.

Printed and published in the U.S.A. by Pauline Books & Media, 50 Saint Pauls Avenue, Boston, MA 02130-3491.

www.pauline.org

Pauline Books & Media is the publishing house of the Daughters of St. Paul, an international congregation of women religious serving the Church with the communications media.

1 2 3 4 5 6   07 06 05 04 03 02

To my dear sister Lisa,
Who dwells in Possibility...

Contents

Foreword

For some it may seem strange to turn to Emily Dickinson, "the belle of Amherst," as a resource for one's prayer life. Is she not the young lady who refused to "accept" Christ as her Savior in her high school years? Is she not the New Englander who, by age thirty, had left the institutional church of her ancestors and had little to do with creed and dogma? Is she not the poet whose apparent individualistic reclusion would seem to have hardly a thing to say about praying to a God who calls creatures to be other-directed?

On closer reading, we find in Emily Dickinson a person searching for truth with a raw honesty that is amazing. She hungered for transcendence, she yearned for fullness of life, she was undaunted in asking the large questions of identity and destiny. Emily Dickinson is a fitting guide for prayer because she *paid attention,* indeed, paid attention with love. Saint John of the Cross, a Doctor of the

Church, maintained that contemplation was essentially "loving attention." Ms. Dickinson practiced this art well and her poetry is an expression of the thoughts and feelings she experienced in her contemplative existence.

Emily Dickinson was a searcher and therefore a questioner. Like the rest of us, she was a struggling pilgrim who pondered deeply the mystery of death, the enigma of suffering, the paradoxes of nature, the ambiguity of life. She refused easy answers; she refused a life of satiation. Like Jacob of the Old Testament, she took on the Divine Wrestler and was willing to be bested.

The books on the life and work of Emily Dickinson are many, but there are none, to my knowledge, that approaches her poetry in terms of prayer. Now we have one and a fine one it is. Fr. John Delli Carpini takes us on a journey of "loving attention" as he shares with us a brief summary of Emily Dickinson's life and then how her poetry speaks to the mystery of God, nature, faith and doubt, and death. More, Fr. Delli Carpini offers six ways of praying poetry and a suggested list of other poets who might be a fitting resource for prayer.

A personal note: Emily Dickinson has been one of my "spiritual directors" for years. When searching for meaning I turn to her poem "If I can stop one Heart from breaking" (included in the volume) and am reminded that to assist others, to be for them like Jesus, provides meaning in life. We are called to service. When the mystery of death troubles my days and nights Emily reminds me (us) that those who love and those who are loved cannot die, for love is immortal. When winter comes and with it that "certain slant of light winter afternoons..." I am called to compassion for all those who suffer depression and despair. I am indebted to Emily Dickinson for the letters she wrote to the world. I am one reader who treasures them and uses them to strengthen my relationship with God.

Poetry is about paying attention; so too prayer. God has sent us prophets and poets. I live with the conviction that one of God's poets is Emily Dickinson. I am convinced that she is both a revealer of Divine wisdom and one who radiates aspects of God's beauty and peace. Fr. Delli Carpini's *Poetry as Prayer: Emily Dickinson* gives us access to this marvelous New England poet and, I dare say, prophet.

✝ Robert F. Morneau
Auxiliary Bishop of Green Bay

Introduction

The results of a *Newsweek* poll taken a few years ago were introduced by the following words—*YOUTH MORE SPIRITUAL THAN RELIGIOUS*. Many people think that spirituality and religion are one and the same, but as the poll showed, this is not the case. Every person has a spiritual component, a yearning for the transcendent, but is not necessarily religious. He or she may even have an active spiritual life, but does not practice his or her religion.

Spirituality is from the Latin word "spiritus" meaning breath or wind. Living a spiritual life is recognizing and responding to God's breath within us. Religion, on the other hand, is the *expression* of one's spirituality, that is, the organization, rituals, and practice of one's beliefs. Religion includes specific conventions, while spirituality is broader. Our cultural knapsack often includes religion along with our looks and ethnic heritage—something like being Italian or Polish. Spirituality, however, is a conscious choice and develops over a lifetime.

One of life's great challenges is to so integrate spirituality and religion that our spirit moves us to worship, while our religious practice intensifies our relationship with God. The headline *YOUTH MORE SPIRITUAL THAN RELIGIOUS* reminds us of how difficult it is to strike a balance between the two. It is often easier to behave devoutly than it is to be sincerely and profoundly holy.

There are many people who are spiritual, but are not necessarily religious. One such person is Emily Dickinson. Her poems express her passionate spirit, her desire to know and love God. She paid much attention to the condition of her inner life, listening and responding to God's breath within and without her, but she avoided doctrine and dogma and, as she grew older, attended fewer and fewer church services. She preferred, instead, to speak with God privately and to ponder life's mysteries in unorthodox ways and places, for example, in her garden among the plants and trees: "It was a short procession, / The Bobolink was there— /," she writes, "An aged Bee addressed us— / And then we knelt in prayer—."[1] Nature was Emily's sanctuary, where, on her knees, close to the earth she loved so deeply, she worshiped God.

I cannot remember who first introduced me to Emily's poetry or when I read my first poem, but I knew at once that I was hooked. In a brief time, I discovered that Emily's "real" life was in her verse, that is, Emily did not write to live, but lived to write. What she saw and heard each day, who she met and what they said were the raw material of her poems, mined, refined, and fashioned in her fertile imagination. Each poem revealed her profoundest thoughts, fears, hopes, joys, losses, and anxieties. "I dwell in Possibility—," she writes, "A fairer House than Prose—." I believe that, through her poems, Emily invited me to understand what inspired her, why she wrote, and how she lived her inner life—to experience, in other words, her creative world.

In the college survey course of American literature that I teach, I wedged Emily's poems between Hawthorne's *The Scarlet Letter* and Melville's *Billy Budd*. We study the poems most often anthologized, especially "I'm nobody! Who are you" and "Because I could not stop for Death." My students are often baffled by her innovative style and put off by her irreverence, but she is always fun to discuss. As a teacher, however, I know Emily only as a poet, an exquisite wordsmith. I read her poems often, even keeping a dog-eared volume in my overnight bag. I take her out at train stations, while stuck in traffic, and on retreat. Emily is always a stimulating and informative traveling companion. "The Truth must dazzle gradually /," Emily advises, "Or every man be blind."[2] Emily has spoken to my heart and head over the years, and allowed me to experience the "Truth's superb surprise."

What is a poet? "This was a Poet—," Emily tells us. "It is That / Distills amazing sense / From ordinary Meanings—." This seemingly simple task is, of course, a gift. A poet sees and hears what most people do not because we often do not look or listen as poets do. In his autobiographical poem *The Prelude*, William Wordsworth writes about his own poetic vocation, a calling with which Emily could certainly identify: "I made no vows, but vows / Were then made for me; bond unknown to me / Was given, that I should be, else sinning greatly, / A dedicated Spirit."[3]

As poet, Emily was also a dedicated spirit. A recluse for most of her adult life in order to compose her poems, she lived intently in the confines of her second floor bedroom, but did not feel imprisoned there. She wrote fondly of the place where, alone and spiritually transported, she composed her almost 2,000 poems: "Of Chambers as the Cedars— / Impregnable of Eye— / And for an Everlasting Roof / The Gambrels of the Sky."[4] Her solitary existence did not restrict the powers of her creative imagination, but allowed them to flow freely like a mountain waterfall.

Emily's poems are about her ordinary life—gardening, reading, family, and friends—but viewed in an extraordinary way through her perceptive and intelligent eyes. "My life has been too simple and stern to embarrass any,"[5] she wrote to Thomas Wentworth Higginson, her literary adviser, editor, and friend. With Higginson as well as other literary and religious figures, despite her reclusiveness, she maintained an active and lively correspondence.

Emily's poems are easy to read, but are not simple to comprehend because they address the many difficult questions we ask each day about life, death, destiny, and God. She was often afraid, mostly of losing family and friends to sickness and death, and so she wrote her poems, she said, for the same reason a boy whistles in a graveyard— to feel less alone.

What does a poet do? "The Poets light but Lamps—," she says, "Themselves—go out— / …. Each Age a Lens / Disseminating their / Circumference—."[6] Poets help us see the world and our true self in a way we have not looked at them before. They do not speak only of their own experience, but the human condition, of which we are sometimes unaware. Poets are often isolated by truth and by their art, as was Emily, but with this consolation: sooner or later, they will somehow touch the hearts of their readers. We all search for truth, but are not always conscious of searching. "From the familiar species / That perished by the Door—," she writes, "We wonder it was not Ourselves / Arrested it—before—."[7] Poets make us more aware of what we are looking for.

As a spiritual poet, Emily guides our search for what is deepest in our soul. She nurtured her spirit as she did her garden, with tenderness and care. She prayed at home and behind closed doors, as Jesus suggested. In a letter to journalist Samuel Bowles, family friend and mentor, she wrote: "We pray for your new health—the prayer that goes not down—when they shut the church."[8] She thought that private prayer was better than public because no one heard it but God.

Emily also prayed for others. She wrote to her cousins when their father died: "Let Emily sing for you because she cannot pray."[9] Perhaps she means, "pray in the traditional way" of her family and ancestors. But, in truth, many of her poems *are* prayers. They are the record of her ongoing dialogue with God. She was comfortable enough to tell God everything, as she could a trusted friend; reading her poems, therefore, is eavesdropping on her holy conversation.

The purpose of this book is to help you to be more attentive to God's breath within you. "Why do you pray?" I asked a cloistered nun. "Because I breathe," she responded. People pray because they want to experience God's extraordinary presence in their ordinary lives. Prayer, therefore, is life; it comes as naturally as leaves to a tree. Prayer is not only reserved for Sunday, but is an unceasing dialogue with God. Even when we sleep, there is communion. God speaks to us in dreams as he spoke to Abraham, Samuel, Joseph, and many others in Scripture.

Poetry and prayer demand a slow and deliberate effort, a dedicated time for reflection, and an authentic response from our soul. Emily worked hard to pack her thoughts; we readers must work hard to unpack them. Her poems can be a stimulus to prayer; the goal, however, is not dissection, but the discovery of our spiritual self within them and, hopefully, the intensification of our relationship with God.

Many poems will resonate with you, but some will not. You will know a poem is yours when, as Emily says, it takes the top of your head off. We may react viscerally to a good poem: our pulse quickens, our temperature rises, and our stomach churns. As a good liturgy that brings us to a moment of worship, an effective poem speaks to the heart with its words, sounds, images, and rhythms. A poem may stir a memory or call us to view the world from a new angle. Reading a poem is a physically, emotionally, and spiritually exhilarating experience.

Emily published a handful of poems in her lifetime. Nonetheless, she wished to entrust her precious words to her future readers:

> Her message is committed
> To hands I cannot see;
> For love of her, sweet countrymen,
> Judge tenderly of me![10]

From her generous hands we accept her kindly gift. Her poems are more than the sum total of her words; they are who she is. And with Emily to lead us, we journey to the springs of life-giving water where we can be refreshed, renewed, and recreated.

CHAPTER I

A Brief Life of
Miss Emily Dickinson

On Visiting Emily's Room in Amherst

She would not want me here—
profane to gad about
the scanty, secret shrine—
her refuge from a world that never knew
the subtleties that graced her thoughts.
Here she lived—but dwelled
within her truer home,
the mansion of her mind,
so amply furnished with her chiseled words.

And there the bed,
the carriage in which
gentle death escorted her
past gazing grain and setting suns.

Now stand I in the nave
Of that blessed church

Where robed in tiffany and lace
She sang the sacred chants
That lavishly anoint my soul.

I wrote this poem in 1996 after my first visit to Emily's home on Main Street in Amherst, Massachusetts. Except for repairs and some renovation, the house has not changed since Emily's family lived there more than a century ago. The Dickinson Homestead originally belonged to Emily's paternal grandfather, but he lost it after suffering bankruptcy. Emily's family continued to live there, however, until her father purchased a home around the corner. Eventually, they returned to Main Street, but not without Emily's protestations about feeling like a pioneer on her way to Kansas. This statement sheds light on how provincial Emily was, living almost her entire life in a very small part of the world.

Much of the Dickinson's furniture has been replaced with reproductions,[1] including Emily's piano on which she improvised at night, but the bed is probably the same one on which she slept and in which she died. Several photographs and paintings of members of her family hang on the walls of the first and second stories, the floors that are now accessible to visitors. Even her gossamer white dress casts a ghostly presence in the room where she composed so many poems.

Emily Dickinson was born in 1830 in Amherst, Massachusetts, and died there in 1886. Her life was relatively uneventful—even for a sleepy, little town in western New England. Except for an excursion to Washington, D.C. and Philadelphia in 1855, and two trips to Boston to consult her eye doctor, she never left the Pioneer Valley. "I never saw a Moor—," she writes, "I never saw the Sea—" For all intents and purposes, Emily led a rather insignificant life. Even in death, she did not travel far; she is buried a stone's throw from her home in West Cemetery.

There is one officially recognized photograph of Emily, a daguerreotype taken when she was about sixteen years old.[2] In it, she is wearing a black dress with a white-laced collar and a ribbon and medallion around her neck. Her arm rests limply upon a table; a closed book is at her elbow. She holds a flower in her hand, perhaps picked from her garden. Her eyes, dark and piercing, gaze beyond the viewer as if occupied by distant thoughts. She did not particularly like the photograph and even denied that it existed. When Higginson asked her for a picture of herself, she sent these words instead:

I had no portrait, now, but am small, like the wren; and my hair is bold, like the chestnut bur; and my eyes, like the sherry in the glass, that the guest leaves. Would this do as well?[3]

Emily belonged to an eminent and privileged Amherst family. Her father, Edward Dickinson, a lawyer and member of congress, was a firm believer in the power of education. He is credited with bringing the railroad to Amherst, possibly inspiring Emily's poem, "I like to see it lap the miles." Emily describes him as "too busy with his briefs to notice what we do.[4] He buys me many books, but begs me not to read them, because he fears they joggle the mind."[5] Edward promised his intended, Emily Norcross, a life of "rational happiness"—not exactly the words of courtly love! A portrait of a scowling Edward hangs in the house. Legend has it that when the painter asked him to smile, he said, "I *am* smiling."

This, however, is not a complete picture. Edward had the capacity for deep emotion below his crusty exterior. It is said that he awakened one morning to a particularly vivid display of the aurora borealis. He was so moved by the phenomenon that he scurried to the church, climbed the campanile and rang the bell to awaken the town. He thought everyone should see the show. Emily's love, devotion, and good humor often melted his heart. Despite his rough edges, she idolized him and, when he died, said there was and would be no one like him again and predicted that the world would be a colder and darker place when he was gone.

Emily's mother, Emily Norcross, was an active member of the Amherst community, best known for her cooking and produce, but not, as Emily wrote, for thought. She makes little mention of her mother in her letters. When Emily was younger, she believed that her mother had failed her; this may or may not be true. "I always ran Home to Awe when a child, if anything befell me," she wrote in a letter. "He was an awful Mother, but I liked him better than none."[6] Emily's statement—"I never had a mother. I suppose a mother is one to whom you hurry when you are troubled"[7]—may be evidence of a strained relationship or, perhaps, a bad day. There is no doubt that her mother was interested in household chores and neighborhood activities, both of which Emily avoided. As time went on, however, Emily tempered her feelings toward her mother with kindness.

Emily was the eldest of three children. Her sister Lavinia was her soul mate, and her brother William, known as Austin, was an intellectual like his father. Even in their later years, the children lived in close proximity. Neither Emily nor her sister Lavinia married. All the children were articulate, but William was also artistic, poetic, and the most public of the three. After they married, Austin and his wife Susan Gilbert lived in the house next door to the Dickinson home. Emily's extended family included her beloved Irish servants and a dog named Carlo.

Emily attended Amherst Academy in 1840 and Mount Holyoke Female Seminary in 1847. I say "attended" because most of what she learned took place outside the classroom. In a letter to Higginson, she wrote: "I went to school, but in your manner of the phrase had no education."[8] This is not to say that Emily did not want to learn. She loved to receive books and possessed a voracious appetite for all knowledge, including science.

In his essay "Self-Reliance" (1841), Ralph Waldo Emerson, the nineteenth-century American essayist and lecturer, writes that "though the wide universe is full of good, no kernel of nourishing corn can come to him but through his toil bestowed on that plot of ground which is given to him to till." Emily probably never read these words, but she lived them every day. Her "plot of ground" was the rich soil of her imagination; the "kernels of nourishing corn" were her poems. On one occasion, her sister

Lavinia commented that Emily was the thinker in the family, spending hours alone digesting a thought. As a citizen of the world of eye and ear, Emily scrutinized the objective world, studying and recording each detail with the patience of a scientist. She writes:

> "Faith" is a fine invention,
> When Gentlemen can *see*—
> But *Microscopes* are prudent
> In an Emergency.[9]

These lines reflect an important dimension of Emily's life—her need to search for certain truth.

Science provided many of the truths that interested Emily, for example, the nature of plants and animals, mathematics and the movement of the stars and planets. The technological developments of the 1830s and 1840s—such as the invention of the sewing machine, telegraph, reaper, and steamboat—fascinated her during her childhood and adolescence. Consequently, many of her poems contain botanical, astronomical, and biological information—the concrete facts of everyday life. "The sailor cannot see the North," she wrote to Higginson, "but knows the needle can."[10] Emily trusted the compass needle because it never lied.

Although she was fascinated by science, religion played a central role in Emily's life and poetry. To better understand why this is so, we must take a closer look at her ancestral religion of Puritanism, which later came to be known as Congregationalism.

Puritanism came to America in 1620 when persecuted English Puritans landed in Plymouth, Massachusetts. With its harsh theological foundation, Puritanism preached the total depravity of the human person, which was completely incapable of instituting or maintaining a right relationship with God by his or her efforts alone. Redemption is solely God's initiative through the power of Christ's death on the cross. The human person remains, however, depraved, "covered over," as it were, by the merits of Christ's sacrifice. The Puritans also believed in the doctrine of predestination, namely, that eternal life is foreordained for some, eternal damnation for others.

As children of the Puritans, the Congregationalists of Amherst were orthodox, evangelical, and highly moral people. Congregationalists believed that they must renounce the world because it could lead to sin. Preaching, mostly solemn and doctrinal, was an art which Congregationalist ministers had mastered thoroughly. The subject of their sermons was often the duty of self-improvement—the

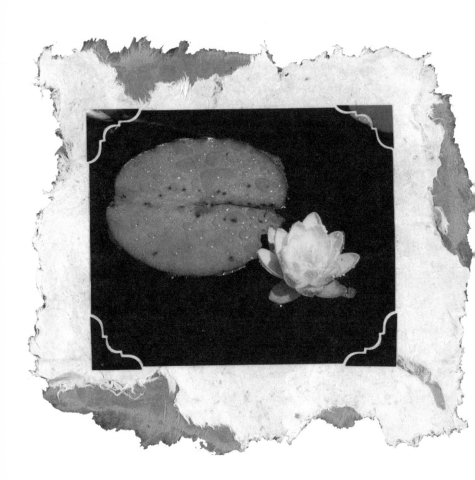

harder one works, the closer one is to the kingdom of God. Leisure, on the other hand, was one of the deadly sins. On one occasion, after a stern sermon on the subject of death and judgment, Emily remarked that the preacher thoroughly frightened her. The subject of perdition, she wrote in a letter, seemed to please him. Religion played an important part in Emily's life in Amherst, where the practice of religion was a public affair and people talked about their faith. At Mount Holyoke Female Seminary, however, Emily refused to publicly declare her Christianity. When Mary Lyon, the president of the school, asked her students to rise if they wished to be Christian, Emily remained seated.[11] She would not compromise herself by doing something to which she had not given sufficient and serious reflection. Nor could she accept the Christ of the Congregationalists, a Christ who viewed this world as merely a stepping-stone to the world to come.

What is significant about Emily's bold behavior is her explanation: "They thought it queer, I didn't rise," she said, "I thought a lie would be queerer."[12] Emily believed that an assent to Christ was also an assent to Congregationalism. She could find little evidence to support the theology of human depravity as she witnessed the decency of the people of Amherst and the faithfulness of friends.

She writes in a poem that,

> Elysium is as far as to
> The very nearest Room
> If in that Room a Friend await.[13]

Instead, Emily chose to be true to her own experience which told her that this life was good and beautiful. Why she viewed the world in her unique way, free from the tyranny of terror as motivation for belief, is a mystery. Led by her imagination and her creative gifts, she dedicated herself to the search for truth as she found it and not as handed on to her by her ancestors.

Later in her life, Emily had several opportunities to claim Christ as her savior and to express her desire to believe, but always withdrew her pledge at the last moment. The rejection of her ancestors' religion was a conscious choice; nevertheless, her decision caused her pain. In a letter, she wrote:

> I am not happy, and I regret that last [school] term, when the golden opportunity was mine, that I did not give up and become a Christian. It is not now too late, so my friends tell me, so my offended conscience whispers, but it is hard for me to give up the world.[14]

This missed opportunity haunted Emily throughout her life, but, as far as we know, she never "gave up" her principles in order to "stand up" for Christ *in a public way.* What happened in her heart and soul, however, remains a secret. Emily chose earth over heaven, at least while she was on it, but, as we will see, it was on earth that she found God. Plagued with what she perceived as a weak faith, she was deeply troubled by the incapacity of her soul to believe as her contemporaries believed: "I am one of the lingering *bad* ones, and so do I slink away, and pause, and ponder, and ponder, and pause, and do work without knowing why—not surely for this brief world, and more sure it is not for heaven—and I ask what this message of Christ means."[15] She searched for the answers within herself and from among those whom she believed could satisfactorily respond to her questions.

Emily also turned to the Bible for solutions, but without much success. The Bible did not hold any special significance for her as it did for the Congregationalists of Amherst, mostly because it was not *her* experience. Despite this, she was familiar with many Bible stories and had her own favorite passages. She mentions several biblical figures in her poetry and addresses a few poems to Jesus, as we will see.

In the end, Emily sought a vision of God that the Congregational Church could not provide. While the progeny of the Puritan religion advocated high morality and the authority of the unadulterated word of God, Emily preferred a more intuitive experience.[16] "Some keep the Sabbath going to Church—," she writes, "I keep it, staying at Home—."[17] "I keep it," she says, not the way her ancestors kept it, but uniquely and personally, and in her own idiosyncratic style. This is where, perhaps, Emily parts company with her Congregationalist contemporaries. She gently critiques the pragmatic religiosity of her churchgoing friends while humorously endorsing her own: "So instead of getting to Heaven, at last— / I'm going, all along." While they "worked" steadfastly for heaven, renounced the world for the sake of the kingdom of God, and enthusiastically confessed Christ as their savior, Emily paused and reflected on what these things meant for her.

It may have been the poetic dimension to religion that Emily found lacking in the Congregationalist Church. But whatever the reason, her rejection of it prevented her from fitting well into the religious society of Amherst. She seemed more interested in the Catholicism of her Irish servants, from whom she gleaned ideas, which she included in several poems.[18] Like Catholics, Emily believed in the innate goodness of people and the universe God created. The world was mysterious and worth pondering. Her poems respect this mystery while honestly admitting the frustration of not understanding it. She plunged headlong into the darkness in order to test her vision. If God made her a thinking, rational being, she believed that she could solve the riddle—although her failure to accomplish this frustrated her even more. Emily attended church services in Amherst until she was at least 25, mostly to listen to the sermons, but she never formally joined the First Church of Amherst where her family worshiped.

Although Emily did not attend church services later in her life, from her letters we know that she was attracted to clergymen, whether for their oratorical skills or intellectual prowess, we cannot be sure. Perhaps the rhetoric caught her attention while the theology stimulated her mind.

Her friendship with Reverend Charles Wadsworth of the Arch Street Presbyterian Church, Philadelphia, for example, lasted a lifetime. Wadsworth was a highly successful, well-known Presbyterian clergyman, happily married, and the father of three. On her visit to Philadelphia in 1855, she heard him preach several times. She tells us in her letters that she was attracted to his eloquent oratorical skills, but we cannot be sure of the chemistry that existed between them; this remains a mystery. Eventually, he left Philadelphia to become the pastor of a church in San Francisco. Other than this meeting with Wadsworth in Philadelphia, Emily saw him only two other times. He visited her in Amherst in 1860 and again in 1880. Despite these brief encounters, separated by decades, many believe she composed her love lyrics for him. He died in 1882 when she was 52.

Several of Emily's poems reflect Wadsworth's ideas or are answers to questions posed in his sermons. When he died, she called him "my closest earthly friend."

Some believe Wadsworth to be the focus of Emily's love. Although she exchanged numerous letters with him over a period of decades, there is no definitive proof that Wadsworth was even aware of her affection for him, if such feelings existed.

Loss and grieving characterized much of Emily's life. Five of her schoolmates died of consumption and were buried in the cemetery near her home. "Perhaps death gave me awe for friends," she wrote to Higginson, "striking sharp and early, for I held them since in a brittle of love, of more alarm than peace."[19] Throughout Emily's life, death was never very far away. Many friends and

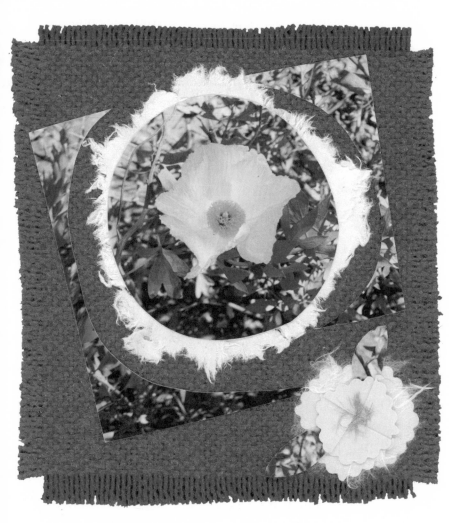

family members died during her lifetime, leaving her shaken and afraid. "Ah! Dainty—dainty Death! Ah! Democratic Death!" she wrote in a letter, "Grasping the proudest zinnia from my purple garden,—then deep to his bosom calling the serf's child!"[20] All this took its toll upon her. In another letter, she expressed her fear of being alone: "Don't leave us long, dear friends! You know we're children still, and children fear the dark."[21] The "dark" is death in whose presence, she says, we call out for help like children.

While at Amherst Academy, at about the age of 11 or so, she experienced the first of the losses that shook her deeply and prompted the questions she would address for the remainder of her life. Leonard Humphrey, the school's principal, died at the age of 23. His death was a revelation to Emily, a shocking recognition of her own mortality. More than just the death of someone she knew, Humphrey's death awakened in her a sense of her own impermanence. It was not only the reality of death that Emily struggled with, but its finality. She wrote to Higginson:

> But I fear I detain you. Should you, before this reaches you, experience immortality, who will inform me of the exchange? Could you, with honor, avoid death, I entreat you sir.[22]

Emily turned to others in her loss and asked for some assurance that death was not the end. She queried Reverend Edward Everett Hale, a pastor in Worcester, Massachusetts, about the "last things":

Please, sir, to tell me if he was willing to die, and if you think him at Home. I should love so much to know certainly that he was today in Heaven.[23]

Emily hoped that her friends were "at Home," but what concerned her more was never "know[ing] certainly." She saw the color of the rhododendron, heard the robin's song, and felt the wet grass, but she could not *know* the immortality of the human soul.

Final and permanent separation from friends and family proved an almost too heavy burden to bear. She admitted to her friend Abiah Root that it was difficult for her to give up the world, so much did she love life, and those connected to it. If death were oblivion, the loss would be forever and this she could not accept: "Parting is all we know of heaven, / " she writes, "And all we need of hell."[24]

It is said that the night is darkest the moment before dawn. The darkness of death all but engulfed Emily, driving her to the brink of despair, but in her poetry she found light. In a letter, she wrote: "I can't stay any longer in a world of death."[25] Eventually, Emily no longer asked "why did they die," but "why am I alive?" Her depression and anxiety surrendered to life and poetic creativity. Searching for answers to her questions became Emily's full-time occupation. Her poems allowed her to experience emotionally what she could not understand intellectually. In the winter of 1861–1862, Emily devoted her life entirely to writing poetry, perhaps a poem a day.

Emily probably read Higginson's article entitled "Letter to a Young Contributor" in the April 1862 edition of *The Atlantic Monthly.* In it, he offered advice to enthusiastic young writers, touching upon themes dear to Emily's soul. He praised writing that can "palpitate and thrill with the mere fascination of the syllables" and extolled the compression of words as a virtue. This letter may have been the spark that ignited Emily's prolific body of work or blew it into full conflagration.

Emily sent several poems to Higginson for his evaluation. She asked him if her poems were alive for the purpose of possible publication, but she did not seem to covet popular recognition as a poet. She feared being turned into a commodity: "I'm Nobody! Who are you?" she asks us. "How dreary—to be—Somebody! How public—like a Frog—."[26] In another poem, she explains:

Publication—is the Auction
Of the Mind of Man—
Poverty—be justifying
For so foul a thing.[27]

Emily preferred instead to live in the seclusion of her room, reflecting, writing letters to family and friends, and crafting her words on odd scraps of paper and napkins. She often tucked a poem in a letter to a friend along with some flower petals from her garden. Like Wordsworth's friend Lucy, who "dwelt among the untrodden ways," Emily's presence made little impression upon the world at large, but to those who knew her, or have come to know her through her poetry, the difference is incalculable.

For the last twenty years of her life, Emily lived in her home with her parents, Lavinia, and their servants. She periodically received guests, but for the most part was quite content to live in her room. "I work in my prison," she wrote to Higginson, "and make guests for myself."[28] She left her room to do the household chores like cleaning and, every so often, to serve her friends her famous black cake and hot tea. The former task was a burden—"I prefer pestilence," she said—the latter, a joy.

"The Soul that hath a Guest," she writes,

> Doth seldom go abroad—
> Diviner Crowd at Home—
> Obliterate the need—[29]

Although Emily composed her poems in her private sanctuary, she read the newspapers and magazines that Austin brought her every day and welcomed any Amherst gossip. She had a fondness for children, perhaps for their sense of wonder and enthusiasm, and often let down home-baked gingerbread from her window on the second floor by means of a pulley system that she constructed.

If Emily were not in her room, she could be found in the family garden, adjacent to the house. There she spent many hours cultivating plants and flowers of all varieties and types. She had a green thumb; consequently, she felt comfortable among the azaleas and daffodils, reflecting and, perhaps, nurturing the seedlings that would later blossom into poems.

By 1870, Emily's life turned sharply inward. She began to absent herself even more from public affairs because they were not, as she said, congenial. She retired almost permanently to her room, and wore only a white dress.[30] Her family was unaware that Emily had made this choice;

they only realized her behavior when friends began to speak to them of their reclusive daughter. I think of Emily's conscious choice of solitude in much the same way that Wordsworth describes the meditative opportunities afforded by a hermitage in "Nuns Fret Not at Their Convent's Narrow Room": "In truth the prison, unto which we doom / Ourselves, no prison is." Emily shut out the world to devote herself entirely to her calling and craft. In "Much Madness is divinest Sense—," she writes about her decision to absent herself from Amherst society: "Demur," she complains, "—you're straightway dangerous— / And handled with a Chain—."

Her detachment from society, however, did not limit her capacity to write on a variety of subjects. Robert Frost said of Emily that she did not need to visit Niagara to write about a waterfall. After she died, Lavinia found hundreds of poems stuffed into a bureau drawer.[31] Many were about places and activities that Emily had neither seen nor done.

Emily was part of her world and yet she was not. There is a tinge of sadness in "This is my letter to the World," almost as if there was no room for a soul like Emily's in Amherst. While her fellow graduates were becoming missionaries and ministers, being good neighbors and, as they said, "improving their mind and character," Emily seemed more interested in a yellow gentian or an approaching storm. She paid close attention to "The simple News that nature told— / With tender Majesty" keeping her eye upon the ordinary, everyday events that most people overlook. Her vocation was to put these feelings and experiences into words—feelings and experiences so deep, so important, and yet so difficult to name, but, nonetheless, experiences that tell the truth in such a way that we cannot live without them.

Emily never experienced what we may call "good health." She suffered from Bright's disease, an ailment characterized by inflammation of the kidney's filtering units. Her condition worsened through her mid-fifties until she was finally confined to bed. Eventually, she fell into a coma. In his diary entry for May 15, Emily's brother Austin wrote:

> It was settled before morning broke that Emily would not wake again this side. The day was awful. She ceased to breathe that terrible breathing just before the whistles sounded for six.[32]

Emily's uneventful life came to a peaceful end on May 15. In her poem "Because I could not stop for Death—," she anticipates the scene of her own funeral:

We passed the School, where Children strove
At Recess—in the Ring—
We passed the Fields of Gazing Grain—
We passed the Setting Sun—

Since then—'tis Centuries—and yet
Feels shorter than the Day
I first surmised the Horses' Heads
Were toward Eternity—.

Emily requested that her body be interred at West
Cemetery, wearing her white dress. As her pallbearers,
the family's six Irish servants carried her coffin out the
back door, around the garden in which she had spent so
many days, through the opened barn, and then across
the grassy field to the family plot. After the mourners
listened to a poem by Charlotte Bronte, Emily was buried in the place where she rests to this day. On her grave-
stone is engraved: *Emily Dickinson, Born December 10,
1830*, and the simple words: *Called Back, May 15, 1886*.
The day after her funeral, the people of Amherst and the
surrounding towns read her obituary in the newspaper:

So intimate and passionate was her love of Nature,
she seemed herself a part of the high March sky, the
summer day and bird-call. Quick as the electric spark

in her intuitions and analyses, she seized the kernel instantly, almost impatient of the fewest words, by which she must make her revelation. To her life was rich, and all aglow with God and immortality. With no creed, no formulate faith, hardly knowing the names of dogmas, she walked this life with the gentleness and reverence of old saints, with the firm steps of martyrs who sing while they suffer.[33]

Her own poem is perhaps a better epitaph:

> Ample make this Bed—
> Make this Bed with Awe—
> In it wait till Judgment break
> Excellent and Fair.
>
> Be its Mattress straight—
> Be its Pillow round—
> Let no Sunrise' yellow noise
> Interrupt this Ground—.[34]

Today, Emily's sister, Lavinia, rests to her right and her father and mother on her left. A single pine bends over the graves. A wrought iron fence now separates the Dickinson graves from the others in the cemetery. On it is engraved: *In Memoriam, Emily Dickinson, Poetess*.

Mabel Loomis Todd published edited versions of Emily's poems in 1890, 1891, and 1896.[35] Emily's niece, Martha Dickinson Bianchi, published another edited version in 1914. But it was not until 1955 that Thomas H. Johnson, the eminent Dickinson scholar, published the first complete collection respecting Emily's unconventional technique. Johnson had the stamina to pour over the almost 2,000 poems in order to decipher Emily's handwriting and quirky style. The publication of the poems by Johnson stirred re-interest in Emily's poetry as well as in her life and times.

In both life and death, Emily never traveled far from the place where she composed her "letter to the World." Reading this long and personal "letter"—the body of poetry she left us—we gain an insight into her active mind and passionate heart. Her questions, doubts, and excruciating losses are ours as well; so too, her poems, her legacy, and joy are now our guide as we journey *our* path toward eternity.

CHAPTER 2

Emily's Poetry
as Prayer

"Lord, teach us to pray." These words express one of the deepest longings of the human heart, the desire to communicate with God. We call this communication *prayer*. There are many ways and places to pray. Thinking of God during a meeting, at a computer terminal, or at a kitchen sink is a prayer. A prayer may be whispered in a car as well as a cathedral, a crowded mall or a peaceful meadow. Note that the basic definition of prayer—lifting our mind and heart to God—says nothing about *what* to say or *where* to say it. What it *does* say is that prayer involves the intellect and emotions, our total being.

Prayer is as unique as each person who prays; this is one of the beauties of prayer. Some pray in a structured way, using a book of spiritual writings or Scripture as a guide. Others prefer to sit silently and wait for the Spirit to move their mind and heart. Some people pray in a church or mosque or temple, while others in a garden, park or on a mountain peak.

We humans are spiritual at our core and our spirit seeks communion with the Spirit from which it originates. "What is born of spirit is spirit" (Jn 3:6), Christ said to Nicodemus who had come to the master pray-er to illumine his mind and heart about the mysteries of the spiritual life.

As we live from day to day, much of life is hidden from our eyes. Even so, we periodically catch glimpses of life's meaning, as a flash of lightning across the sky illuminates the landscape for a moment. Prayer helps us to process these insights, because when we pray we quiet the mind, heart, and soul. We listen to what we cannot hear when drowned by the noise of everyday life. Even Jesus did this; he left the crowd to spend time in communion with God. He invited his disciples to join him in an "out of the way place" so they could recharge their spiritual batteries. When they returned from the mountains, they had a fresh perspective and a new resolve. Hopefully, this is true of us as well. Prayer keeps the channels open between ourselves and God.

Emily prayed often, mostly in her garden or her room. She mentions in several letters that she prayed for others; she sometimes even slipped into a letter a line or two of comforting verse, the "balsam word" as she called it, if those she wrote to were ill or experiencing some other pain. Several of her poems are prayers addressed directly to God or are about God; in others, Emily addresses the suffering Jesus, in whom she found a friend. Jesus, she believed, knew her pain: the loss of friends in death and her struggle to believe. "At least to pray is left / is left / Oh Jesus in the Air!" she prays. "I know not which thy chamber is / I'm knocking everywhere."[1] She even wrote a poem about praying,[2] where she says that prayer is simply getting God's attention in order to express our experiences of beauty, pain, fear, and joy.

Above all, Emily pondered the mystery of God when she prayed, that is, she was aware of and responded to God who dwelled within her and in the natural world. Among the flowers and the trees, she sensed a presence which interfused all things. She saw evidence of God in the movement of the leaves, the sweetness of a bird's song, and the starry canopy above. She observed God in the lilies of the field and the birds of the air, as Jesus had directed. Nature was a holy place for Emily, an emblem of transcendence; God was truly present everywhere, not only in heaven, as some of her religious friends believed.

Maintaining faith in God, however, was never easy. Her human fear of loss, abandonment, loneliness, and death shook her faith in a providential and benevolent

God; this, however, did not prevent her from praying: "The Martyr Poets—did not tell—," she writes, "But wrought their Pang in syllable—."[3] With little or no expectations, she told God exactly what she thought and felt. Somehow, prayer fixed in her a moment of clarity at the center of life's agitation, or as Frost defines a poem, "a momentary stay against confusion." Whenever Emily found this kind of faith, she discovered a valuable treasure.

Emily possessed a poetic gift that helped her to see and hear the world uniquely, as most people do not. She writes:

> The Only News I know
> Is Bulletins all Day
> From Immortality.
>
> The Only Shows I see—
> Tomorrow and Today—
> Perchance Eternity—
>
> The Only One I meet
> Is God—The Only Street—
> Existence—This traversed
>
> If Other News there be—
> Or Admirabler Show—
> I'll tell it You—

As we see from this poem, the spiritual world was important to Emily. The ultimate answers to her questions about "Immortality," "Eternity," "God," and "Existence" lay beyond the grave. "Secrets stapled there," she writes, "Will emerge but once—and dumb— / To the Sepulchre—."[4] She believed her poetic responsibility was to report to us, her readers, whatever puzzles she solved.

In her poems, and in various ways, Emily frequently asked God why she was alive. Some poems express a stoic patience when God does not answer; others are the screeches of a child when she does not hear what she expects. In every case, however, her poetic mission was to express the truth she suffered painfully to discover. Each poem, even each word, bears the mark of her mental agony, the spiritual anguish she endured while attempting to find a clue to the mystery of life.

Her brief poems—the longest is fifty lines—have an almost immediate impact on the reader. She packs each word and phrase with meaning, the pure density I imagine a black hole to be like. Higginson wrote about what a good poet was able to do:

Oftentimes a word shall speak what accumulated volumes have labored in vain to utter: there may be years of crowded passion in a word, and half a life in a sentence.[5]

Emily agrees. "Essential oils are wrung," she writes about the crucible of the poetic process, "The attar from the rose / Is not expressed by suns alone, / It is the gift of screws."[6] Because Emily experienced many losses, mostly through death, her poems are often about the human emotions of grief, loneliness, pain, and frustration. She found a creative "gift of screws" even in her painful and potentially destructive human experiences.

Emily is not a traditional poet. She was an innovator, choosing poetic methods that were startling: the use of dashes for emphasis, irregular meters, imperfect rhymes and grammar. But this odd inventiveness has earned her a reputation as one of America's most original poets. Like our own prayer that is often confused, spontaneous, and emotional, Emily's poems express a spiritual force that cannot be measured or contained.

In Emily's poetry, there is little theological jargon, even less doctrine and creed, but much about God and human existence. God was a mystery to Emily, a riddle wrapped in an enigma, as was human life, especially her own. Emily asked many questions about life and death and she often turned to God for answers. The carefully chosen words of her poems helped her to formulate her questions and express her ideas.

Emily prayed to understand; how much she came to understand, if anything, we will never know. But this did not discourage her from praying. She persevered in prayer, especially when her faith was weak. In fact, at such times she expressed her most intense longings and persistent doubts. She was not afraid to tell God what she thought and felt. In a humorous and spontaneous burst at the end of "Besides the autumn poets sing," she writes: "Grant me, Oh Lord, a sunny mind— / Thy windy will to bear!"

Above all, Emily is a visionary. The immediacy of her vision and her inventive expressions lend a spontaneity to her prayers, like an on-going conversation with God, interrupted only by a meal or a visit from a friend. In sharing her vision with her readers, it is as if poet and reader discover the truth simultaneously. Her poems, therefore, demand a visionary reading, an acceptance of the mystery that she addresses in her poems. Analysis is not required and, in fact, to be avoided. If you find yourself stuck on a word or confused by a phrase as you pray, move on. Do not attempt to tame her; Emily will not be domesticated. Success is in allowing the poem to master you. The discovery of a poem's elusiveness is reward enough. If the poem is a mystery, let it be the mystery of God.

Reading Emily's poems is an emotional and intellectual experience. Her verse stirs our heart and stimulates our mind, but above all, invites us to ponder the ultimate questions of love, life, and death, the fonts from where we draw our prayer. At the heart of Emily's prayer is the desire to know God. As with human friendship, we know God more intimately when we speak our mind, open our heart, and listen to his voice. Somewhere in this process, there is communication. In her poem about praying, she writes: "They fling their Speech…in God's Ear / If then He hear—."[7] God's deafness did not stop her; rather, it forced her to shout the louder.

A common fear we have when we pray is "not doing it right," not praying correctly. We are afraid that God will not hear our prayer or that our prayers do not work. But really, there is no "right way" to pray; different people pray in different ways, "flinging their speech" at God and discovering that prayer comes from their individual and personal relationship together. Prayer can be as simple as a word or two directed to God or as complex as we feel it needs to be.

God knows what we need before we ask. Trying to do too much too quickly will only end in frustration and feelings of defeat, like trying to lose fifty pounds in a week, or to quit smoking in a day. To us who experience the challenge of praying, Emily says, "keep it simple!" Be satisfied with your prayer and move on; tomorrow is another day.

Emily's struggle is a human struggle. Every day she reflected on the many questions that we all ask: Who is God? Why am I alive? Will I live forever? Emily's almost 2,000 poems address many themes and a variety of topics. I have selected and categorized several poems for the purpose of our prayer, with the topics "God," "Nature," "Prayer," "Faith and Doubt," and "Death."

Writing poetry was not a pastime for Emily; it was a vocation. She foresaw the time when future readers would benefit from her struggle: "That when [the poets'] mortal name be numb— / Their mortal fate—encourage Some—."[8] We are the beneficiaries of her profound insights and her struggle to believe.

CHAPTER 3

Emily and God

Discovering God is a lifelong adventure. The journey begins when we first hear God's name and will end when we meet God face to face. The path to God, however, is not straight. It meanders over hills and through valleys, traverses through dark forests and across sunny meadows. We may become distracted and frustrated when we make little progress, but as Saint Catherine of Siena said, the journey to God *is* God.[1] We are not only traveling *to* God; we are discovering God all along the way. This is because God meets us personally, in the ordinary events of our day. Elizabeth Barrett Browning writes that "Earth's crammed with heaven / And every common bush afire with God."[2] But we can overlook God if we are not conscious seekers. Browning continues, "But only he [or she] who sees, takes off his shoes / The rest sit around it, and pluck blackberries." Discovering God is searching deliberately and consciously in "every common bush."

Emily desired to discover God; she tried each day to find God and wrote about what she discovered in her poems. Although Emily's poems reflect *her* journey, they also speak to us.

WHERE THOU ART—THAT—IS HOME—

> Where Thou art—that—is Home—
> Cashmere—or Calvary—the same—
> Degree—or Shame—
> I scarce esteem Location's Name—
> So I may Come—
>
> What Thou dost—is Delight—
> Bondage as Play—be sweet—
> Imprisonment—Content—
> And Sentence—Sacrament—
> Just We two—meet—
>
> Where Thou art not—is Woe—
> Tho' Bands of Spices—row—
> What Thou dost not—Despair—
> Tho' Gabriel—praise me—Sir—

Emily savored her private moments with God; "Just We two—meet," she says. In this poem, she asks no questions, makes no demands, but simply enjoys the pleasure of being "at home" with God as she valued the presence of a close friend. "Home" is not a place: "I scare esteem Location's Name." Home is wherever God is: "Where Thou art—that—is home—."

The concept of "home" was important to Emily, representing sanctuary, acceptance, and security in the unpredictable world of "Bondage," "Imprisonment," and "Sentence." Ironically, Emily felt freer in her home than outside it. She wrote in a letter of October 1851: "Home is a holy thing—nothing of doubt or distrust can enter it's (sic) blessed portals."[3] At home, she was at liberty to do what she enjoyed: play the piano, entertain guests, and write her poems. In God, she tells us, she found that same security and contentment. Even when things changed and life was confusing, God remained the same.

On the other hand, Emily feared God's absence; she did not want to be alone: "Where Thou art not—is Woe—" and "What Thou dost not—Despair—." Even the angel Gabriel's assurance that God was with her, as God had been with the Virgin Mary, was no consolation to Emily. She needed to "feel" God's presence in her blood and bones.

This poem says much about the way Emily prayed and how she imagined God. Prayer was not so much something Emily *did* or *said* as who she was: a person attuned to the spiritual world and open to its meaning. Her prayer, therefore, was a response to these intimations.

For Emily, God was a friend, an essential and indispensable person in her life. She wanted to be with God, as one person thinks of the other and seeks his or her company. And like good friends, Emily is content to be silent with God. With God, as opposed to friends and family, she could be present at anytime or in any place. Because God is not confined to a church or to heaven, but is everywhere, "So I may come." Nor did Emily think she had to feel necessarily *religious* when she was with God. Rather, Emily expresses a familiarity with God, a friendship as intimate as any human friendship, and, perhaps, even more.

UNTO ME? I DO NOT KNOW YOU—

"Unto me?" I do not know you—
Where may be your House?

"I am Jesus—Late of Judea—
Now—of Paradise"—

Wagons—have you—to convey me?
This is far from Thence—

"Arms of Mine—sufficient Phaeton[4]—
Trust Omnipotence"—

I am spotted—"I am Pardon"—
I am small—"The Least
Is esteemed in Heaven the Chiefest—
Occupy my House"—

This poem is based on a passage from John 1:35–42 in the New Testament. One day, Jesus noticed that John the Baptist's disciples were following him. "What are you looking for?" he asked them. "Rabbi, where are you staying?" they replied. "Come, and you will see." The evangelist tells us that the disciples stayed with Christ through the afternoon.

Emily asks Christ the same question, but with different words: "I do not know you— / Where may be your House?" "Come, and you will see," Christ invites her. But she wonders how she will get there: "Wagons—have you—to convey me? / This is far from Thence." Christ tells her that his embrace is all she needs, and confidence in God's power to transport her: "Trust Omnipotence," he commands. Even so, Emily is reluctant and feels spiritually unprepared to go. To her, "I am spotted," Christ responds, "I am Pardon." Emily's "I am small" prompts her "the last shall be first" in God's kingdom.

Christ's words must have been a comfort to Emily who believed that she had betrayed him. Her refusal to "stand up" for Christ at Mount Holyoke Female Seminary caused her heartache throughout her life. She experienced a deep sense of shame, loss, and frustration for not accepting Christ into her life. "Unto Me? I do not know you—," however, reflects not so much Emily's desire to be with God as it does God's invitation to fall into the embracing arms of love. Emily experienced the warmth of that embrace when she opened herself to God's presence because she believed that the suffering Christ understood every human pain—even hers. She wrote about Christ's compassion in a letter of 1884:

> When Jesus tells us about his Father, we distrust him. When he shows us his Home, we turn away, but when he confides to us that he is "acquainted with Grief," we listen, for that also is an Acquaintance of our own.[5]

The compassionate Christ responds to Emily's anxiety with peace, her alienation with acceptance, and her

frustration with love. The poem is Emily's belief that there would be a place *even for her* in God's house.

SAVIOR! I'VE NO ONE ELSE TO TELL—

> Savior! I've no one else to tell—
> And so I trouble *thee*.
> I am the one forgot thee so—
> Dost thou remember me?
> Nor, for myself, I came so far—
> That were the little load—
> I brought thee the imperial Heart
> I had not strength to hold—
> The Heart I carried in my own—
> Till mine too heavy grew—
> Yet—strangest—*heavier* since it went—
> Is it too large for *you*?

In her later years, Emily chose to live her life apart from society. She enjoyed the company of her family, and periodically, her friends who visited her home; but for all intents and purposes, she lived alone. Emily lived as a recluse because she preferred thought to anything else; quiet places fired her imagination and created the atmosphere to write her poems. For this reason, among others, only a few people understood and appreciated what she was about;

there were even less with whom she could converse. Many people called her the "Myth of Amherst," and she was sometimes the object of clothesline gossip. She often found herself not so much alone as lonely in her poetic calling, wondering about issues that few bothered with or had time to address. Perhaps this is her state of mind when she shouts: "Savior! I've no one else to tell— / And so I trouble *thee*." Her words express the frustration of being misunderstood and misinterpreted. But God, she knew, above all, would understand: "Dost thou remember me?" Deep in her heart, she knew that the answer was "yes."

The most common form of prayer is petition; people pray because they are in need. Throughout the gospel, Jesus invited his disciples to ask, beseech, plead, invoke, entreat, and cry out. In "Savior," Emily does exactly that: "I brought thee the imperial Heart / I had not strength to hold—." She carries her heart to Christ, heavy with unspecified cares, and obviously not for the first time; she has been in this position before. Perhaps she bears the petitions of a friend or family member for whom she promised to pray, or the need may be her own. In either case, poverty of one form or another is present.

Emily's prayer of petition expresses an awareness of and desire for God's help. People and the circumstances of life sometimes disappoint and betray us, but when we pray, we are conscious of a presence beyond the fickleness of human nature and the unpredictability of life. In her times of need, Emily counted on God's "presence." Her poem expresses the spiritual truth that the prayer of the drowning person is perhaps the most sincere because it emerges from the most desperate vulnerability.

FOREVER AT HIS SIDE TO WALK—

Forever at His side to walk—
The smaller of the two!
Brain of His Brain—
Blood of His Blood—
Two lives—One Being—now—

Forever of His fate to taste—
If grief—the largest part—
If joy—to put my piece away
For that beloved Heart—

All life—to know each other—
Whom we can never learn—
And bye and bye—a Change—
Called Heaven—
Rapt Neighborhoods of Men—

Just finding out—what puzzled us—
Without the lexicon!

In this poem, Emily writes that she and God share one mind and one heart: "Brain of His Brain— / Blood of His Blood—." Her words echo those of Genesis where God creates Eve: "This at last is bone from my bones," says Adam, "and flesh from my flesh" (2:23). Although God and she are "Two lives," they are "One Being" in the same way husband and wife are one spirit while remaining unique individuals. In a marriage, a couple shares a common life; but they also share life's challenges, thus growing individually as persons and together as a couple. This is also true when we pray. We come as we are to God, speaking honestly and from our heart. Over time, our relationship with God intensifies.

"His fate," that is, Christ's death on Calvary, is also Emily's crucifixion: her losses, loneliness, abandonment, pain, and struggle to believe and accept her own mortality. She wondered if, when death arrived, she could place her spirit in God's hands as Christ did from the cross. But she also suffered less spiritual, more practical concerns. She would have liked her poems to be published, but refused to alter her unique and innovative style to meet a publisher's prescriptions. No wonder her grief is large and her joy so small.

Like a healthy marriage, a spiritual relationship with God develops over a lifetime, despite the challenges it encounters. In fact, the adversities of life often heighten love and trust. Although Emily discovered something new about God each day, she admitted her frustration in not knowing God entirely and apart from nature. Only death would reveal the final answer to the questions she continually pondered each day: "Just finding out—what puzzled us— / Without the lexicon."

HEAVEN HAS DIFFERENT SIGNS—TO ME—

"Heaven" has different Signs—to me—
Sometimes, I think that Noon
Is but a symbol of the Place—
And when again, at Dawn,

A mighty look runs round the World
And settles in the Hills—
An Awe if it should be like that
Upon the Ignorance steals—

The Orchard, when the Sun is on—
The Triumph of the Birds

When they together Victory make—
Some Carnivals of Clouds—

The Rapture of a finished Day—
Returning to the West—
All these—remind us of the place
That Men call "Paradise"—

Itself be fairer—we suppose—
But how Ourself, shall be
Adorned, for a Superior Grace—
Not yet, our eyes can see—

The psalmist writes that the heavens silently speak the glory of God. Emily would agree: "'Heaven' has different Signs—to me—." Each unique moment: dawn, noon, and sunset; and every part of creation: orchard, birds, and clouds, revealed to her another facet of God's glory. God was a tangible presence for Emily, not only a spirit. She looked for God among the things she knew.

Why does Emily say that "All these—remind us of the place / That men call 'Paradise'"? The Congregationalists taught that God lived in heaven, which was where the predestined would go after death. Emily, however, saw paradise reflected on earth. Heaven above would "be fairer," she admits, but earth is our only experience of life, at least for now. Perhaps Robert Frost says it best: "Earth's the right place for love: / I don't know where it's likely to go better." What will happen later, Emily says, remains a mystery: "But how Ourself, shall be / Adorned, for a Superior Grace— / Not yet, our eyes can see—."

Emily's final thought reflects her feelings of being spiritually unprepared to meet God. She felt ostracized from the religious community, in part, because she would not publicly accept Christ. And she must have wondered if Christ would shun her because she preferred an earthly paradise to a heavenly one. But as Emily listened to her heart, she rebelled against the idea that all this natural beauty had no ultimate purpose.

Emily's life was a journey of discovery. Engaging nature, she said, was a sure and certain way of finding God. But Emily saw more than God's beauty in the colors of the sunrise and the first light of dawn. She saw God's "mighty look" upon the world, a glance that sparked in her a yearning to probe the mystery and a desire to know God more completely: "An Awe if it should be like that / Upon the Ignorance steal—." The brilliance of the sun-drenched hills, the sound of a flock of birds, the rolling clouds, and the setting sun reflected God's glory, not in and for themselves, but for what they inspired in her soul, a quickening of faith and an experience of God's presence.

I KNOW THAT HE EXISTS

I know that he exists.
Somewhere—in Silence—
He has hid his rare life
From our gross eyes.

'Tis an instant's play.
'Tis a fond Ambush—
Just to make Bliss
Earn her own surprise!

But—should the play
Prove piercing earnest—
Should the glee—glaze—
In Death's—stiff—stare—

Would not the fun
Look too expensive?
Would not the jest—
Have crawled too far?

As a child, Emily most certainly played the game of hide and seek with Austin, Lavinia, and their friends in the yard and fields around their home. It was a child's game and all in good fun, but as an adult, playing the same game with God was another matter with more serious implications. Emily looked for God, but finding him was never easy: "He has hid his rare life /," she writes, "From our gross eyes." God was "other," a spiritual being beyond the comprehension of her finite mind. But signs of God were everywhere; discovering these clues made the game interesting: "Just to make Bliss / Earn her own surprise."

Emily experienced an unquenchable desire to enlarge her vision and to know the ultimate meaning of her life. As a rational person, she longed for answers about her destiny. This, in some way, accounts for her ongoing quest for God, a pursuit that was often difficult and disorienting. Yet despite the challenges, she continued to seek the unfailing source of eternal value. Although there were times of disillusionment and discontentment on this great religious odyssey, she worked at finding meaning in the seemingly ordinary events of her day. And sometimes, when she looked, God was recognizable, although silent and invisible.

Emily learned to live each day within the mystery of unknowing. She realized that she could never completely find what she was looking for. She played the game, but did not expect to win, at least not in this world. When she died, she would finally find the God she had searched for all her life, not behind tree or rock, but plainly, in full sight. "Should the glee—glaze— / In Death's—stiff—stare— / Would not the fun / Look too expensive?" By then, it was no longer a game, but serious and, finally, eternal business.

CHAPTER 4

Emily and Nature

"But the Lord was not in the wind...not in the earthquake...not in the fire. After the fire there was a tiny whispering sound. When he heard this, Elijah hid his face in his cloak and went and stood at the entrance of the cave" (1 Kgs 19:11–13).

Noise and confusion, the social "earthquakes" and "fire" of everyday life, can affect our sanity and health. People and daily circumstances make demands that sometimes cause us to forget what is important. We may want to prioritize our lives—to eat well, exercise, pray, and experience God's "tiny whispering sound"—but we sometimes lose our resolve and fall back into old patterns. Seeking a place of quiet, however, helps to create an environment where our spirit can catch up to us. Like food and water for our body, our soul needs solitude and a comfortable place for its spiritual nourishment.

The natural world was Emily's place for reflection. Amid the hills and fields that surrounded Amherst, she maintained a sense of childlike wonder and exhilaration even as an adult. Amazed at the beauty of the created world, she never tired of what she had seen and heard the day or even the hour before. Emily spent many hours with nature, her sanctuary of harmony and joy; there she found spiritual and emotional peace. Her poems reflect nature's sights and sounds with the most affectionate language. She captures every detail, from the way a snake parts the grass like a comb through hair to the multiple colors of the setting sun.

Nature sometimes quieted her soul and helped her to prioritize her values; at other times, it enlivened her spirit. In 1862, for example, she tried, and failed, to write a poem about a hummingbird. She decided that the final piece was awkward, and put it aside. Eighteen years later, she returned to the poem, editing the original twenty lines down to eight and calling it "A Route of Evanescence." Thomas H. Johnson, the editor of *Final Harvest: Emily Dickinson's Poems*, said about the poem: "She never forgot what she wanted to express about the hummingbird…Sound, iridescent color, vibration." But in order to create a great masterpiece about a tiny bird, she had to look long and hard. This she did with almost everything, attentive to and perceptive of the world around her.

More important than how Emily observed nature was how nature affected her. Among the plants, trees, animals, and stars, she experienced a presence that transcended the changing seasons and varied moods of the human heart. More than philosophy or theology, nature taught her that, despite its inaccessibility, truth existed and could be known, if only partially.

When Higginson asked her who her friends were, Emily responded:

> Hills, sir, and the sundown, and a dog large as myself, that my father bought me. They are better than beings because they know, but do not tell.[1]

Nevertheless, Emily spent a lifetime asking, seeking, and knocking. She had many questions, and nature provided some of the answers. Her poems reflect what she learned. Where she sang of nature's mystery, she provided us with an insight into and an appreciation of this unspoken wisdom. Nature invited Emily to enter its mystery. Consequently, as often as she sought answers among the trees, flowers, and plants of her garden, she had another question.

For those who wish to travel this path with Emily, the muse may be the local park, a walk in the woods, or a hike along a mountain trail. The wise king Solomon said:

It is he who gave me unerring knowledge of what exists, to know the structure of the world and the activity of the elements…for wisdom, the fashioner of all things, taught me (Wis 7:17, 22).

The poet, Wallace Stevens, would agree: "Perhaps the truth depends upon a walk around a lake."

BRING ME THE SUNSET IN A CUP

Bring me the sunset in a cup
Reckon the morning's flagons up
And say how many Dew,
Tell me how far the morning leaps—
Tell me what time the weaver sleeps
Who spun the breadths of blue!

Write me how many notes there be
In the new Robin's ecstasy
Among astonished boughs—
How many trips the Tortoise makes—
How many cups the Bee partakes,
The Debauchee of Dews!

Also, who laid the Rainbow's piers,
Also, who leads the docile spheres

By withes of supple blue?
Whose fingers string the stalactite—
Who counts the wampum of the night
To see that none is due?

Who built this little Alban House
And shut the windows down so close
My spirit cannot see?
Who'll let me out some gala day
With implements to fly away,
Passing Pomposity?

Every sunrise and sunset was an unrepeatable event for Emily, as if God had created each particular day only for her. "Bring *me* the sunset in a cup," she asks (italics mine). The poem expresses the unbridled enthusiasm and playful self-centeredness of a child in a candy store, wide-eyed, questioning incessantly, and wanting everything in sight.

Emily's enthusiasm is contagious. Caught up in a litany of nature's sights and sounds, each new image flashes a mental picture of experiences we have had, but sometimes have failed to fully understand or appreciate. Her rhetorical questions, "Tell me how far the morning leaps— / …what time the weaver sleeps," challenge us to accept the mystery of what we do not know.

Job in the Old Testament experienced this mystery as well. After God explained to him the wonders of creation, Job responds with these words:

> I know that you can do all things and that no purpose of yours can be thwarted. Therefore I uttered what I did not understand, things too wonderful for me, which I did not know. I had heard of you by [word of mouth], but now my eye sees you (Job 42:2–5).

Like Job, Emily desired an intuitive experience of God; she, too, had heard of God from others' "word of mouth," but wanted to see and hear God with her own eyes and ears. This she did in her garden; there, she not only saw flowers, plants, and insects, but the objects created by a Divine Artist. When she looked upon his handiwork, the profound beauty crafted in every detail, she saw him.

"Bring me the sunset" overflows with exotic imagery that takes our breath away: morning leaps, a weaver sews the pieces of the sky together, flora and fauna are in ecstatic motion. There is activity everywhere. Emily draws our attention to a world we have often seen with our eyes, but rarely with our souls. She says that her vision is limited, however, catching only a fraction of nature's meaning, so rich and full is the created world. But this does not discourage her. Like a curious child, she charged ahead and asked about how and why things worked.

Emily wanted answers to her questions. Not being able to grasp the full truth caused her moments of frustration. "Who built this little Alban House," she writes, "And shut the windows down so close / My spirit cannot see." Emily ached for the "Truth's superb surprise," but had to be content with being dazzled only gradually.[2]

The natural world provides us with a place to rest and see; our spirit cannot do without it and expect to live. Even Jesus escaped to the mountains or the wilderness to pray, particularly after a stressful experience. He invited his disciples to join him in an "out of the way place." We, too, are invited to quiet our inner self and allow the colors, aromas, and sounds of nature to speak and open us to a presence beyond ourselves. When we hear God's "tiny whispering sound," we find peace.

If life is in the details, then Emily helps us to pay attention; she invites us to stop and examine the delicate color of a butterfly, listen to a cheerful robin's song, and feel awed by the majesty of the setting sun. No day is too hectic to find our place in the universe and to make ourselves aware of who and where we are. These brief encounters with created beauty may help us find the inner peace that subsists at the heart of agitation.

THESE ARE THE DAYS WHEN BIRDS COME BACK—

These are the days when Birds come back—
A very few—a Bird or two—
To take a backward look.

These are the days when skies resume
The old—old sophistries of June—
A blue and gold mistake.

Oh fraud that cannot cheat the Bee—
Almost thy plausibility
Induces my belief.

Till ranks of seeds their witness bear—
And softly thro' the altered air
Hurries a timid leaf.

Oh Sacrament of summer days,
Oh Last Communion in the Haze—
Permit a child to join.

Thy sacred emblems to partake—
Thy consecrated bread to take
And thine immortal wine!

Nature also taught Emily the harsh lesson of life's finality. This poem is Emily's ode to autumn, the season of nature's dying. By the end of fall, most birds have migrated south, she tells us, in anticipation of the harsh, New England winter. A few remain, however, to reminisce of summer's joy and the days of nature's plentitude. The cold and snow have not set in; the sky is blue and the air still mild, but winter is not distant despite the "old sophistries of June." Nature tempts Emily to believe that the later flowers and warm days of Indian summer will last into the winter months: "Almost thy plausibility / Induces my belief."

Like the few birds that remain, Emily also "take[s] a backward look," not only upon the days of summer, but upon her life. Soon, a cooler and more ominous wind disturbs the scene. The "timid" leaves eventually die and fall reluctantly to earth, but this, she knows, is their fate. In this dying, however, there is life. The seeds are promises of a new birth, the immortal wine of new existence: "Oh Sacrament of summer days, / Oh Last Communion in the Haze—."

Emily found comfort in these reflections on mortality, because they helped her to appreciate the moment. They also stirred in her an anticipation of what surprises the future had in store. Now, however, she is held in suspense, hoping for her *final* "communion." These are her memories, the "sacred emblems" of summer days and the holy bread and wine of nature's store.

NATURE IS WHAT WE SEE—

"Nature" is what we see—
The Hill—the Afternoon—
Squirrel—Eclipse—the Bumble bee—
Nay—Nature is Heaven—
Nature is what we hear—
The Bobolink—the Sea—
Thunder—the Cricket—
Nay—Nature is Harmony—
Nature is what we know—
Yet have no art to say—
So impotent Our Wisdom is
To her Simplicity.

Emily learned much from children, whom she believed possessed insight into life and a freedom of behavior that adults relinquish as responsibilities increase. One of these children was Austin's son, Gilbert. Her nephew Gilbert died when he was nine, stirring in Emily the deepest grief and most tender emotions. In a letter to her sister-in-law, Susan, Emily wrote:

Gilbert rejoiced in Secrets—His Life was panting with them—With what menace of Light he cried "Don't tell, Aunt Emily"! Now my ascended Playmate must instruct *me*. Show us, prattling Preceptor, but the way to thee![3]

The simplest lessons of life are often the most profound.[4] And children sometimes teach these lessons to adults.

In "'Nature' is what we see—," this is the case. Emily attempts to dissect nature's sights and sounds, but fumbles when she realizes that no words or thoughts can fully disclose nature's secrets. "Nature is what we know—," she writes, "Yet have no art to say." Only a child perceives this, a child who enjoys the pleasures of nature in and for itself, and for no other purpose. Emily surrenders to nature's mystery like a child rather than attempt to solve or analyze it like an adult.

Emily honored her emotions with the highest respect, trusting implicitly the gentle affections that led her deep within herself and into the nature of things. Here she discovered a presence beyond the comprehension of her intellect. She took to heart the critical importance of learning nature's simple lesson: "One impulse from a vernal wood, / Can teach you more of man, / Of moral evil and of good, / Than all the sages can."[5]

If I can stop one Heart from breaking

If I can stop one Heart from breaking
I shall not live in vain
If I can ease one Life the Aching
Or cool one Pain

Or help one fainting Robin
Unto his Nest again
I shall not live in Vain.

Emily found rest and comfort in the natural world, but nature was also therapeutic—soothing her spirit, quieting her anxious heart, and even healing her body. She also offered this therapy to those who were ill, visualizing the power of nature and sending it to those who needed help. She wrote to Bowles:

Can't I bring you something? My little Balm might be *o'erlooked* by wiser eyes—you know—Have you tried the Breeze that swings the Sign—or the Hoof of the Dandelion? I own 'em—Wait for *mine!*[6]

Emily believed in the healing powers of the written word; she sometimes included poems in her letters, hoping that her verse would cure a headache or mend a broken heart. This mission of healing helped Emily to find meaning in her life: "If I can ease one Life the Aching / Or cool one Pain… / I shall not live in Vain." In reflecting on nature's generosity to her, and giving something back, she found purpose and a reason to be alive.

CHAPTER 5

Emily and Prayer

Prayer is ultimately about love: God's love for us and our return of love for him. This friendship, like any human friendship, is not so much about knowing God as it is about meeting God in affection and understanding. Friendship, says the sixteenth-century poet and mystic Saint John of the Cross, is when two people attain "boldness with each other." When we have touched another's life deeply and he or she has touched ours, we can be "bold" in asking for help, seeking each other's presence without needing a reason, and sharing our feelings without embarrassment. The philosopher Martin Buber speaks of friendship in terms of "I" and "thou": my "I" or the person I am, meets your "thou" or the person you are. This kind of "presence" is also true for our relationship with God. God is never distant from us, and so we do not pray to make God present to us, but to make our "I" present to God's "Thou."[1]

God was as present to Emily in her garden as in a church; but in her garden, Emily was more open to God. Her "I" was attuned to God's animating spirit, which she believed existed in the natural world around her. In nature, Emily opened herself honestly and authentically to God; there, she was able and ready to offer her full attention.

Prayer is not an activity apart from who we are and what we do, it *is* who we are and what we do. This is why Saint Paul says to pray unceasingly, that is, to be conscious of a presence beyond and outside of ourself, yet within our self, at all times and in all places. It is possible, therefore, to pray wherever we are, as we walk, work, shop, cook, and even as we sleep and dream. Prayer is not always speaking words, but is often a silence that acknowledges mystery.

Emily was almost always open to God's mystery. Consequently, she did not desire to *get to heaven*, so much as to *go to heaven* each day. In fact, when Emily sat in her garden, she believed that she *was* in heaven. There she spoke to God and God spoke to her, "I" to "Thou" and "Thou" to "I." In ordinary daily events and the created world she observed each day, she encountered the infinite.

My period had come for Prayer—

My period had come for Prayer—
No other Art—would do—My Tactics missed a
rudiment—
Creator—Was it you?

God grows above—so those who pray
Horizons—must ascend—
And so I stepped upon the North
To see this Curious Friend—

His House was not—no sign had He—
By Chimney—nor by Door
Could I infer his Residence—
Vast Prairies of Air

Unbroken by a Settler—
Were all that I could see—
Infinitude—Had'st Thou no Face
That I might look on Thee?

The Silence condescended—
Creation stopped—for Me—
But awed beyond my errand—
I worshipped—did not "pray"—

In this poem, Emily tells us of her struggle to pray. "Period," "Art," and "Tactics" all suggest the formality of those who approach prayer as a structured methodology for communicating with God. Emily sets out in this manner, telling us of her plan to discover the God who "grows above": "And so I stepped upon the North / To see this Curious Friend—." She cannot find this God because he has no home or address, but lives in "Vast Prairies of Air." Emily, however, continues to search: "Infinitude—Had'st Thou no Face / That I might look on Thee?"

In the last stanza Emily finds an answer to her question: "The Silence condescended— / Creation stopped— for Me—." In the end, she discovers that God does not live in any particular place, but is a universal, spiritual presence in the world and beyond the world. Halted by this revelation, she can find no words, but can only worship in silence—an appropriate response to meeting God.

Unceasing prayer is not ritualized, nor are there words. It is a constant state of an awareness of oneness with God, a sincere seeking for the good with a faith that it is attainable. When Emily opened herself to the wonder of nature, her spirit was moved to respond in devotion. Her prayer was not so much a speaking to God as an experiencing of God's presence in the world.

OF GOD WE ASK ONE FAVOR

> Of God we ask one favor,
> That we may be forgiven—
> For what, he is presumed to know—
> The Crime, from us, is hidden—
> Immured the whole of Life
> Within a magic Prison
> We reprimand the Happiness
> That too competes with Heaven.

Emily included this poem in a letter to her friend, Helen Jackson, who had injured her foot in an accident. "Knew I how to pray," Emily wrote, "to intercede for your Foot were intuitive, but I am a Pagan."[2] What thoughts and feelings accompanied this statement?

Emily's childhood influences taught her that her body imprisoned her soul; eventually, her spirit would escape at death. Earthly life was a vale of tears to endure with patience; her real "life" would be with God in heaven after death. Emily's "Crime," therefore, was enjoying what she should have resisted; her "sin" was not desiring heaven more than the paradise she found outside her door.

As a child, what Emily learned from her parents and teachers was not her own day-to-day experience. To her, nature was beautiful, pleasing to eye and ear. She wrote to Thomas Higginson:

> When much in the Woods, as a little Girl, I was told that the Snake would bite me, that I might pick a poisonous flower, or Goblins kidnap me, but I went along and met no one but Angels, who were far shyer of me, than I could be of them, so I haven't that confidence in fraud which many exercise.[3]

When she sat among the trees or moved about the garden, Emily experienced an indescribable happiness. This caused great conflict in her heart: "Immured the whole of life / Within a magic Prison / We reprimand the Happiness / That too competes with Heaven." In the end, she pled guilty as charged to loving her life too much, and chose to meet God in this world rather than wait until the next. She was, nevertheless haunted by guilt, which caused her to fear she would never be worthy enough to reach the place prepared for those who loved God. She concluded her letter to Helen Jackson by asking: "May I once more know, and that you are saved?"

OF COURSE—I PRAYED—

> Of Course—I prayed—
> And did God Care?
> He cared as much as on the Air

A Bird—had stamped her foot—
And cried "Give Me"—
My Reason—Life—
I had not had—but for Yourself—
'Twere better Charity
To leave me in the Atom's Tomb—
Merry, and Nought, and gay, and numb—
Than this smart Misery.

This poem reveals how distant Emily felt herself to be from the comfort of formal prayer. She stands on the precipice of despair, suffering the anguish of God's cold shoulder: "Of Course—I prayed— / And did God care?" In a letter to her friends, Doctor and Mrs. Holland, Emily wrote: "If prayers had any answers to them, you were all here tonight, but I seek and I don't find, and knock and it is not opened."[4] Because Emily regretted her decision to reject Christianity, she sometimes agonized over the possibility that, in the end Christ would ignore her as she thought she had ignored him. She felt abandoned and scorned, and in her deep despair over her inability to pray, even preferred non-existence: " 'Twere better Charity / To leave me in the Atom's Tomb— / …Than this smart Misery."

Is there any more authentic prayer than the prayer of a wounded soul? In this poem, Emily's frustration is her prayer. She expresses her "boldness" with God, that is, her open and tormented heart, bursting with pain and desire. More positively, Emily is able to share her feelings with God as she would a trusted friend.

The desolation we sometimes experience when we feel God's absence is, ironically, the powerful desire for God's presence. To fall in love with God, says Saint Augustine, is the greatest of all romances and to seek God is the greatest adventure. Emily invites us to tell God how we feel, to express our deepest longings, to seek God among the things we know, and to pray even when we think God is not listening. Sometimes, the most important part of prayer is what we experience, not what we say; we often spend a great deal of time telling God what we think should be done, and not enough time waiting in the stillness for God to tell us what to do.

Saint Augustine reminds us that finding God is the greatest human achievement. And so it is important to keep trying. Eventually we may find God where we least expect—in the darkness of surrender and in the depths of abandonment.

To hear an Oriole sing

> To hear an Oriole sing
> May be a common thing—
> Or only a divine.

It is not of the Bird
Who sings the same, unheard,
As unto Crowd—

The Fashion of the Ear
Attireth that it hear
In Dun, or fair—

So whether it be Rune,
Or whether it be none
Is of within.

The "Tune is in the Tree—"
The Skeptic—showeth me—
"No Sir! In Thee!"

Emily's life was not what many would consider event-
ful. The birds, hills, and trees that surrounded her were a
constant source of joy and pleasure and each day opened
like another chapter in a mystery novel, a story that she
eagerly awakened to devour. While some grow accustomed
to the common events of the day either because of rou-
tine or because they live, as Thoreau says, "lives of quiet
desperation," Emily experienced each new day afresh.

For Emily, every sight and sound, no matter how often she saw or heard them, was extraordinary. In this

poem, she acknowledges the "ordinary miracle" of the bird's song: "To hear an Oriole sing / May be a common thing— / Or only a divine." It is extraordinary because we believe it to be so: "So whether it be Rune, / Or whether it be none / Is of within."

Emily expressed this important idea in a letter to Higginson: "I think you would like the Chestnut Tree, I met in my walk. It hit my notice suddenly—and I thought the Skies were in Blossom."[5] Emily found a wealth of meaning in her daily experiences and was open to nature's intimations, the simplest elements dazzled her with un-imaginable ecstasy and moving her to respond in prayer. "The 'Tune is in the Tree—'" is the skeptic's credo, she says, if one hears only with his or her ears. The believer, on the other hand, also listens with his or her heart.

During our times alone with God, walking or sitting in receptive silence amid the beauty around us, we may be inspired. With receptivity and silence, we open ourselves to receiving God and may (quite suddenly) find ourselves at prayer.

CHAPTER 6

Emily's Faith and Doubt

Defined theologically, faith is belief in God and the intellectual acceptance of Revelation's truth. Faith is not only doctrine and dogma, it is also trusting a person, developing a loving relationship that is tested over time and purified in the crucible of trial and error. "Do not let your hearts be troubled. You have faith in God; have faith also in me" (Jn 14:1), Jesus instructed his apostles. Eventually, as they spent more time with him, the apostles grew to trust Jesus. Their faith increased as he showed them how much he loved them and invited them to love him in return.

"I do believe," said the father of the boy possessed by a demon, "help my unbelief" (Mk 9:24). *Help our unbelief*...this is our prayer as well. Faith does not walk alone; it is often accompanied by its shadow: doubt. The spiritual life is a journey of faith *and* doubt, belief *and* unbelief, taken one step at a time. Faith and doubt are circular, like the *ouroboros*, the image of the snake which bites its own tail. Doubt leads to faith and faith to doubt again throughout the course of our spiritual lives.

Emily lived comfortably within this circle of faith and doubt, saying, "we both believe and disbelieve a hundred times an hour," she kept an ever-watchful eye on "that religion / That doubts as fervently as it believes." Doubting was a blessing for Emily because it kept faith nimble.

Emily often wrote about her experience of faith and doubt. She asked many questions and sometimes received answers. Emily cherished her faith. She also cherished her doubt because it challenged her belief. If Emily showed us only her faith, we would know only half her soul. But because she also reveals to us her doubt, we find in her a sympathetic friend.

To lose one's faith surpasses

> To lose one's faith surpasses
> The loss of an estate,
> Because estates can be
> Replenished,—faith cannot.
>
> Inherited with life,
> Belief but once can be;
> Annihilate a single clause
> And Being's beggary.

Emily was often anxious, worrying about the health and general well-being of family and friends. She wrote to those who were ill and tried to comfort them with her words. She feared losing those she loved because she feared being left alone. Material possessions were of no help at such times; faith, however, brought her solace and comfort. "Faith is the assurance of things hoped for," says the author of the Letter to the Hebrews, "the conviction of things not seen." (11:1) When her mother died, Emily wrote to her cousins, expressing a remarkable faith in "things not seen":

> I believe we shall in some manner be cherished by our Maker—that the One who gave us this remarkable earth has the power still farther to surprise that which He has caused.[1]

More than anything she owned, faith was Emily's most valued possession; in fact, without her faith, she considered herself destitute. Faith allayed her fears and helped her to surrender her anxiety to a Presence that she felt kept a watchful and providential eye on her.

MY FAITH IS LARGER THAN THE HILLS—

My Faith is larger than the Hills—
So when the Hills decay—

My Faith must take the Purple Wheel
To show the Sun the way—

'Tis first He steps upon the Vane—
And then—upon the Hill—
And then abroad the World He go
To do His Golden Will—

And if His Yellow feet should miss—
The Bird would not arise—
The Flowers would slumber on their Stems—
No Bells have Paradise—

How dare I, therefore, stint a faith
On which so vast depends—
Lest Firmament should fail for me—
The Rivet in the Bands.

Emily loved life, the natural world around her, and
her family and friends who gave her great joy. Despite
the promise of endless happiness in heaven, she preferred
what she knew to the unknown. Emily was not naive.
Through the years, she witnessed the deaths, some un-
timely, of many people who were close to her. Their deaths
made her realize the brevity of all life, including her own.

In the first part of this poem, Emily tells us how much she wants her life to last: "So when the Hills decay— / My Faith must take the Purple Wheel / To show the Sun the way—." If the sun does not rise in the morning, she says, the birds will not sing or the flowers bloom. Emily will do everything in her power to prevent the sun from not rising, even claiming that she will pilot the chariot that carries the sun around the earth herself.

By the end of the poem, however, Emily realizes the importance of faith on so many levels: "How dare I, therefore, stint a faith / On which so vast depends." Emily accepts her insignificance, but also understands that what is not seen is far more important than what is seen. In this poem, sustained by the unending energy of the universe, she is propelled by the power of faith and bathed in the light of eternal wisdom.

Emily believed that the sun would rise in the morning and that her spirit would not die "when the Hills decay." Faith helped her to see beyond the apparent finality of death and to anticipate, as Hamlet says, the "undiscover'd country from whose bourne / No traveller returns."[2]

Emily's preoccupation with death did not lead her to despair, but sharpened her vision and helped her to appreciate the gift of life. Emily's was a practical faith that she experienced each day and not merely at a Sunday morning church service. Just as she believed that the sun would rise, Emily trusted that God would not refuse to let her spirit live forever.

In this poem, Emily takes the leap of faith and the risk that trust involves. We also do this each day as we place our faith in the returning dawn and the cycles of nature. Faith in a providential and benevolent God involves a similar risk.

WE GROW ACCUSTOMED TO THE DARK—

> We grow accustomed to the Dark—
> When Light is put away—
> As when the Neighbor holds the Lamp
> To witness her Goodbye—
>
> A Moment—We uncertain step
> For newness of the night—
> Then—fit our Vision to the Dark—
> And meet the Road—erect—
>
> And so of larger—Darknessess—
> Those Evenings of the Brain—
> When not a Moon disclose a sign—
> Or Star—come out—within—

The Bravest—grope a little—
And sometimes hit a Tree
Directly in the Forehead—
But as they learn to see—

Either the Darkness alters—
Or something in the sight
Adjusts itself to Midnight—
And Life steps almost straight.

Emily longed to explore her doubts; her passion was to discover a reality beyond her senses. She spent much time, however, feeling her way through spiritual darkness. In this poem, Emily writes that, as we walk the spiritual path, we adjust ourselves to doubt: "When Light is put away—." The "Light" here is the light of faith. We must continue to move ahead even when there is no light, becoming "accustomed to the Dark" of life's mysteries and unanswered questions. When our eyes finally focus, we advance, unsure of our way, but moving forward nonetheless.

Emily calls these periods of doubt "Evenings of the Brain," when life does not make sense and all seems hopeless and bleak. These are the times, says Emily, to keep walking even without the light of faith to illumine our steps: "The Bravest—grope a little— / And sometimes hit a Tree." We learn to walk in the dark of doubt and acclimate ourselves to the surroundings by groping through the darkness. Emily did this often as she pondered the questions of pain, suffering, loneliness, and the loss of those she loved.

Although we walk by the light of faith, we must also negotiate the dark of doubt on the spiritual journey. During these times, it is good to remember that God is also in the darkness. What we seek with groping fingers may not be very far away.

How brittle are the Piers

> How brittle are the Piers
> On which our Faith doth tread—
> No Bridge below doth totter so—
> Yet none hath such a Crowd.
>
> It is as old as God—
> Indeed—'twas built by him—
> He sent his Son to test the Plank,
> And he pronounced it firm.

In Congregationalist Amherst, doubters were few, at least in public. However, Emily expressed her doubts without shame. "In a Life that stopped guessing, you and I should not feel at home,"[3] she wrote to her sister-in-law. Her many questions were catalysts for reflection and even prayer. She went so far as to thank God for her doubts because they stripped away her false assumptions and invited her to find fresh reasons to believe. In this way, her faith was always new.

Emily tells us in this poem that believing is risky business, like walking a perilous bridge over a deep gorge; there is always the danger that the bridge will collapse, spilling us into the abyss. Peter learned this lesson when Jesus invited him to walk toward him on water. Peter walked confidently until he realized where he was.

This is our experience as well. Safely in the boat, we will not drown, but we miss the opportunity to trust God. In order to believe, we must leave the safety of the boat, we must cross the tottering bridge. Emily says that this is the way God wants it: "It is as old as God— / Indeed— 'twas built by him—." God invites us to leave the boat and walk on the waters of faith, to leave the firm ground and cross the bridge of faith—the waters and bridge that lead us to God.

Emily learned to depend on her faith as she did upon her many other resources. She discovered that faith was not a promise to never fall, but an assurance that she was supported, *even when she was falling*. Without something outside herself to believe in, she had only herself left to believe in.

THIS WORLD IS NOT CONCLUSION

This World is not Conclusion.
A Species stands beyond—
Invisible, as Music—
But positive, as Sound—
It beckons, and it baffles—
Philosophy—don't know—
And through a Riddle, at the last—
Sagacity, must go—
To guess it, puzzles scholars—
To gain it, Men have borne
Contempt of Generations
And Crucifixion, shown—
Faith slips—and laughs, and rallies—
Blushes, if any see—
Plucks at a twig of Evidence—
And asks a Vane, the way—
Much Gesture, from the Pulpit—
Strong Hallelujahs roll—
Narcotics cannot still the Tooth
That nibbles at the soul—

This poem is Emily's creedal statement, an articulation of her belief in God and in God's promises. She does not use her familiar dashes in the first line, but a period, declaring the absolute certitude of her belief: "This World is not Conclusion"...*period!* She "concludes," therefore, that the world is not the end. This expression of her faith did not come easily. It took shape in her soul through many hours of painstaking and deliberate reflection. It was not blind, but rather a surrender of the need for physical proof and an openness to discover something new, which sometimes involved a process of trial and error: "Faith slips—and laughs, and rallies—."

The traditional ways of knowing are futile here, "Philosophy—don't know,"—because there is no human answer to the riddle, at least not on this side of life. Emily does not believe because *others* believe; her faith is a response to a felt invitation to search for something greater than herself, an inducement she cannot refuse: "Narcotics cannot still the Tooth / That nibbles at the soul—." At the heart of this restlessness, she experienced an inexplicable presence, "Invisible, as Music—," she writes, "But positive, as Sound." This music invited her to enter its mystery and to discover a reality beyond the physical world. The delicate lilies, the industrious bees, and the lofty hills were emblems of something greater: the Power who fashioned them.

THE SOUL SHOULD ALWAYS STAND AJAR

> The Soul should always stand ajar
> That if the Heaven inquire
> He will not be obliged to wait
> Or shy of troubling Her
>
> Depart, before the Host have slid
> The Bolt unto the Door—
> To search for the accomplished Guest,
> Her Visitor, no more—

Emily was always open and anxious to understand the mystery of God. "The Only News I know," she writes in another poem, "Is Bulletins all Day / From Immortality." For this reason, Emily spent time alone in order to listen. These "bulletins," however, are fleeting glimpses of truth that, as Emily writes, are here today, but gone tomorrow.

Emily's ability to view the world like a child made every day a new surprise. She cherished what she could not understand, and in this way, she kept open the lines of Divine communication. With this attitude, she accepted the eternal quality of those things she could not comprehend, but longed one day to understand.

Faith is a belief in things that our senses have not experienced, our mind have not understood, but that we have touched in other ways and have accepted as true. God communicates with us constantly, Emily tells us, awakening in us an awareness of Divine revelation. Such revelations come, not from extraordinary events, but through the daily and ordinary experiences of life if our hearts are open. "The Soul should always stand ajar" when these revelations of faith come so we may "admit" them.

Emily writes that spiritual vigilance is vital to a life of faith and doubt. We may be startled by beauty, lifted by forgiveness, or buckled by pain and loss. God can be subtle, gently placing in our path the signs that can open our eyes; or God can be forceful, allowing us to reach the brink of desolation. We must be ready for all these experiences, or risk missing the wealth of meaning they hold for us.

CHAPTER 7

Emily and Death

The year 1851 had been one of many deaths in Amherst. A number of young people perished from various diseases, especially consumption. Moreover, Austin and others upon whom Emily leaned for support were away. Not surprisingly, she was often frightened, baffled, and full of questions. She wrote in a letter to her brother: "It *cannot* be—yet it is so…one and another, and another—how we pass away!"[1]

It is no wonder, then, that Emily became preoccupied with the process of dying. She began paying close attention to natural signs of decay: crumbling walls, fallen trees, and birds that, so vibrant a week before, were now gone. She reflected on this in a letter to Higginson:

> When a little girl, I had a friend who taught me Immortality; but venturing too far himself, he never returned. Soon after my tutor died, and for several years my lexicon was my only companion. Then I

found one more, but he was not contented I be his scholar, so he left the land.[2]

She wrote in another letter: "To live, and die, and mount again the triumphant body, and *next* time, try the upper air—is no schoolboy's theme!"[3] Distressing thoughts of death forced Emily to reflect upon the meaning of her life, and, together with her own deteriorating health, became sober reminders of her own mortality. "There's been a Death, in the Opposite House, / As lately as Today—," she writes, "I know it, by the numb look / Such Houses have—always—."[4]

I NEVER LOST AS MUCH BUT TWICE

I never lost as much but twice,
And that was in the sod.
Twice have I stood a beggar
Before the door of God!

Angels—twice descending
Reimbursed my store—
Burglar! Banker!—Father!
I am poor once more!

Emily wrote this poem around 1858, after several of her friends had died: "Twice have I stood a beggar / Before the throne of God." So close to home, these deaths shook her to her core, as indicated in a letter to Mr. and Mrs. Holland: "Say is [death] everywhere? Where shall I hide my things? Who is alive? The woods are dead. Is Mrs. H. alive? Annie and Katie—are they below, or received to nowhere?"[5]

During that year, Emily often found herself in a growing state of panic. Why was she losing her friends? What purpose was there in making new acquaintances, only to have them die? God seemed, indeed, a "burglar," robbing her of what she held dearest to her heart. She wrote in a letter to her cousin: "We, too, are flying John—and the song 'here lies,' soon upon lips that loved us now—will have hummed and ended."[6] Over and over, Emily experienced her impoverished state.

The loss of family and friends in death can be a devastating blow to the spiritual life—or it can be a blessing. Emily wisely expressed her deepest emotions, avoiding "the grief that does not speak / Whispers the o'er-fraught heart, and bids it break."[7] Emily's heart *did* break time and again, but the experience of the death of loved ones also gradually helped her understand her own powerlessness and fragility. Loss is an invitation to review priorities and values and to place our hope in a higher presence. Often, in the acceptance of loss, new life is discovered.

TO DIE—TAKES JUST A LITTLE WHILE—

To die—takes just a little while—
They say it doesn't hurt—
It's only fainter—by degrees—
And then—it's out of sight—

A darker Ribbon—for a Day—
A Crape upon the Hat—
And then the pretty sunshine comes—
And helps us to forget—

The absent—mystic—creature—
That but for love of us—
Had gone to sleep—that soundest time—
Without the weariness—

As with other major events, death always causes a stir in a small town; everyone knows when someone has died. Emily attended many funerals, mostly those of family and friends, but even the death of a stranger interested her. This poem, like several others, reflects her first-hand knowledge of what happens when someone dies.

First, a gathering of watchers wait for the last breath ("only fainter—by degrees"); after death, there is the wake and funeral service (the "darker Ribbon"); and finally, the interment of the deceased person ("the soundest time—/ Without the weariness—"). After death, life goes on: "And then the pretty sunshine comes—/ And helps us to forget—." Although she grieved, Emily accepted the reality of death as the last chapter of the book of a person's life. She was sometimes able to find some humor in death. Writing about a friend who died twenty years before, she said: "My earliest friend wrote me the week before he died 'If I live, I will go to Amherst—if I die, I certainly will.'"[8]

Not only was Emily able to cope with death, but also to bring peace and consolation to others. After the death of her uncle, Loring Norcross, Emily wrote his family a letter of comfort: "The grief is our side, darlings, and the glad is theirs."[9] In a sense, Emily began to see that the unembodied side of life is already here in another dimension; the two worlds intermingle. While she could only be aware of *her* world, those who had gone ahead were aware of *both:* "The absent—mystic—creature— / That but for love of us—." She could think of them and they could think of her.

When we confront death in a realistic and positive way, we appreciate our life; each day, each moment is more precious. This wisdom does not come without a price, however; facing death head-on is frightening, but indispensable if we are to be fully alive and human.

AFRAID! OF WHOM AM I AFRAID?

> Afraid! Of whom am I afraid?
> Not Death—for who is He?
> The Porter of my Father's Lodge
> As much abasheth me!
>
> Of Life? 'Twere odd I fear [a] thing
> That comprehendeth me
> In one or two existences—
> As Deity decree—
>
> Of Resurrection? Is the East
> Afraid to trust the Morn
> With her fastidious forehead?
> As soon impeach my Crown!

Emily wrote about death in more than 500 of her poems. Sometimes, she looked at death scientifically, at other times more personally. In either case, she gradually learned to live with death.

In the playful poem, "Afraid! Of whom am I afraid?", Emily shares several insights that she gained through her observation and reflection on the deaths of family and friends. Death is the only way to pass from this life to the next, the "Porter of my Father's Lodge." Her words remind us of Saint Paul: "What you sow is not brought to life unless it dies" (1 Cor 15:36). Emily realized that she would never reach "those great countries in the blue sky of which we don't know anything" unless first she died. She also understood that life is not to be feared but a gift to be cherished and enjoyed. Despite its fragility, Emily appreciated life, and not even death could rob her of that pleasure.

Resurrection is a matter of faith. Although there is no guarantee that the sun will rise each morning, Emily lived believing it would: "Is the East / Afraid to trust the Morn / With her fastidious forehead?" And so it is with the afterlife; there was little need for Emily to question redemption; she believed herself saved, but did not make a display of her certainty. She wrote: "Do not try to be saved—but let Redemption find you—as it certainly will—Love is it's (sic) own rescue, for we—at our supremest, are but it's trembling Emblems—."[10]

There is beauty and consolation in these simple words, a proud declaration of life, a humble recognition of mortality, and an assured confidence in the promises of providence.

TIE THE STRINGS TO MY LIFE, MY LORD

Tie the Strings to my Life, My Lord,
Then, I am ready to go!
Just a look at the Horses—
Rapid! That will do!

Put me in on the firmest side—
So I shall never fall—
For we must ride to the Judgment—
And it's partly, down Hill—

But never I mind the steepest—
And never I mind the Sea—
Held fast in Everlasting Race—
By my own Choice, and Thee—

Goodbye to the Life I used to live—
And the World I used to know—
And kiss the Hills, for me, just once—
Then—I am ready to go!

Almost all fear is fear of the unknown, and death is
the greatest unknown. Gradually, however, we discover
that death is a process of letting go, a reluctant willing-
ness to embark on a voyage to an unknown world. No

one wants to die, says Emily, but the adventure that awaits us in that "undiscovered country" is enough to at least arouse our interest.

Emily imagines herself dying or already dead in several poems, perhaps because she did not want to be surprised when death finally arrived. In this poem, she tells God that she is ready to die: "Tie the strings to my Life, My Lord, / Then, I am ready to go!" As she does in "Because I could not stop for death," she here imagines that final journey in a horse-drawn carriage. Although she did not know where she was going, she was certain that judgment would be a stop along the way.

Emily expresses no apparent fear of death in this poem because, as she says, God is her companion: "Held fast in Everlasting Race— / By my own Choice, and Thee—." After one last glance at everything she loved on earth— nature, family, and friends—she does her best to say goodbye. Yet, she is not quite able to turn away: "And kiss the Hills, for me, just once." Finally, she looks ahead to what awaits her: "I am ready to go!"

I SHALL KNOW WHY—WHEN TIME IS OVER—

I shall know why—when Time is over—
And I have ceased to wonder why—

Christ will explain each separate anguish
In the fair schoolroom of the sky—

He will tell me what "Peter" promised—
And I—for wonder at his woe—
I shall forget the drop of Anguish
That scalds me now—that scalds me now!

Emily believed that when she died God would answer her many questions; life's mysteries would no longer baffle her. The mystery of death is arguably the most important subject we grapple with and, at the same time, one about which we know nothing from firsthand experience. The wisest of sages throughout the centuries of human existence were not able to unravel it. Neither does Emily attempt to unravel it in this poem. She looks at death as the beginning of the life that awaits her beyond the grave, a life free from anguish and pain, and especially, the frustration of not knowing the answers. Death speaks to Emily of possibility, of eternal destiny in a place where there are no more questions and every tear will be wiped away.

THERE CAME A DAY AT SUMMER'S FULL

There came a Day at Summer's full,
Entirely for me—

I thought that such were for the Saints,
Where Resurrections—be—

The Sun, as common, went abroad,
The flowers, accustomed, blew,
As if no soul the solstice passed
That maketh all things new—

The time was scarce profaned, by speech—
The symbol of a word
Was needless, as at Sacrament,
The Wardrobe—of our Lord—

Each was to each The Sealed Church,
Permitted to commune this—time—
Lest we too awkward show
At Supper of the Lamb.

The Hours slid fast—as Hours will,
Clutched tight, by greedy hands—
So faces on two Decks, look back,
Bound to opposing lands—

And so when all the time had leaked,
Without external sound

Each bound the Other's Crucifix—
We gave no other Bond—

Sufficient troth, that we shall rise—
Deposed—at length, the Grave—
To that new Marriage,
Justified—through Calvaries of Love—

On April 16, 1862, Emily sent Higginson four of her poems, and she began her introductory letter by asking: "Are you too deeply occupied to say if my verse is alive?"[11] Higginson responded by asking her many personal questions and offering a critique of her poems, which prompted her to write on April 25: "Thank you for the surgery—it was not so painful as I supposed."[12] With this second letter, she sent several more poems, one of which was "There came a Day at Summer's full." Was her inclusion of this poem an attempt to find meaning in her present suffering, to see resurrection beyond her experience of Calvary?

Indeed, she wrote this poem in the spring of 1861, which had been particularly difficult for Emily. She had said to goodbye to several friends: Wadsworth, her clergy friend from Philadelphia; Samuel Bowles, journalist and family friend; and her first tutor, Benjamin Newton. Perhaps she feared that each separation forebode another, or that she would never see her friends again. Although a painful experience, absence sometimes does makes the heart grow fonder.

Emily felt uncertain as she wrote to Higginson for the second time. What would he think of her verse? What would he think of *her?* She had rarely been so forthright with a stranger, but she probably needed to unburden her pain. Her inclusion of "There came a Day at Summer's full" with her highly personal letter, which reflected many anxious moments over the death of family and friends, her deteriorating eyesight, family squabbles, etc., testifies to her familiarity with loss.

However, the poem, is also about life and reunion. Despite the recurrent pain of parting that year, Emily rejoices in the grandeur of nature. The first full day of summer banishes the winter doldrums and the New England spring chills, promising a change for the better: "As if no soul the solstice passed / That maketh all things new—." The brilliant sun, colorful flowers, and soft breezes lifted her above her cares and transported her to nature's sanctuary where she felt safe and secure.

The poem begins with a brief description of a perfect day. As in other poems that we have seen, Emily envisions this "gift" as solely hers, a day "for the Saints." June 22 is the summer solstice, the longest day of the year—the day with the most light and least darkness. She cherishes every moment of light, every hue of flower and sky and hill, and every summer aroma. Nature is sacramental, the "Wardrobe—of our Lord—," that is, the outward display of God's exquisite raiment. As one is hushed by the majesty and splendor of the arches and vaults of a great cathedral, Emily is silenced in the presence of the natural architecture around her: "The time was scarce profaned, by speech— / The symbol of a word / Was needless." The sacredness of the moment would not be spoiled by any utterance of words. As so often before, here in the bright, sunny cathedral of air, flowers, and trees, Emily encounters God.

Emily is concerned, however, with the encroaching night: "The Hours slid fast—as Hours will, / Clutched tight, by greedy hands—." She knows that, be it her friends or nature, everything changes, nothing lasts. Even the glory of this day will end and so will her encounter with God. But here is where Emily's transformation begins. Although she anticipates her own end, her mystical vision goes beyond the darkness of the night to a day that will not end: "And so when all the time had leaked, / Without external sound / Each bound the Other's Crucifix— / We gave no other Bond— / Sufficient troth, that we shall rise—." Emily looks beyond the night to what she hopes lies beyond, an eternal nuptial with God and with everyone who had been taken from her: "Deposed— at length, the Grave— / To that new Marriage, / Justified—through Calvaries of Love."

In this final meeting, which Emily hopes will be an experience of resurrection, is actually the ultimate sacrament, the mystical marriage of her human soul and the Divine Spirit. As in every sacrament, heaven unites with earth to create a graced moment, an encounter with the living God. At this moment, "Where Resurrections— be—," Emily will be one with Christ. "So faces on two Decks, look back, / " she writes, "Bound to opposing lands." She believed herself headed in the "wrong" direction, that is, away from Christ. Yet she recognizes one point of reference: her identification with Christ's suffering on the cross in her pain of rejection, loneliness, and loss.

We cannot help but think that the moment of reconciliation will be even sweeter for Emily who once publicly denied Christ as a schoolgirl. She believes that she has paid the price for this denial in the many "Calvaries of Love," that more than warrant her entrance into new life. If heaven is the reward for those who have suffered for love, as did Christ, Emily believes Christ, the bridegroom, will welcome her "To that new Marriage."

In this poem, Emily reveals the depths of her soul, her fears and longing, her hopes and dreams, her faith and doubt. Although she had traveled this bumpy road many times before, in "There came a Day at Summer's full," she anticipates the everlasting day of heaven when, at peace and reconciled to God, Emily reaches her final destination to claim the prize of glory.

GIVEN IN MARRIAGE UNTO THEE

Given in Marriage unto Thee
Oh Thou Celestial Host—
Bride of the Father and the Son
Bride of the Holy Ghost.

Other Betrothal shall dissolve—
Wedlock of Will, decay—
Only the Keeper of this Ring
Conquer Mortality—

CHAPTER 8

Six Steps to Reading Poetry in a Holy Way

1. Open Your Eyes!

Look at the words on the page. Examine the poem before you read it. What shape is it? Read the words with hungry eyes. Devour their meaning. Look for anything unusual. Decide which words or phrases are meaningful to you. Read them again. Jot them down and look at them later. Share them with a friend. Look at the poem at another time of day, in another light, by a fire, in the rain, or in the middle of the night when you cannot sleep.

A poem may help you get in touch with God. Prayer broadens and deepens the channel that already exists between yourself and God, and a poem will often help you to get started.

2. Open Your Ears!

Listen to the sound of the poem's words. Read the poem aloud. Read it with full voice. Read it softly. Listen to its music. Have someone read the poem to you. Read it to him or her. Read it while listening to music. Does the poem rhyme? What sounds do you like? What sounds are harsh? Savor the words like good wine; let them roll on your tongue. What words are repeated? Are they long or short? Listen to the poet reading his or her own poem if you can. Do any words or phrases sting you, make you think, or cry? Can you describe your feelings to someone else? To a spiritual director?

Although it is possible to pray on the run, everyone needs time dedicated only to God. Step aside from the mainstream of your activity and, with a quiet place and tranquil mind, give your ears to God.

3. Open Your Nose!

There is a legend that when God created Adam, he made his nose first. Through his nose, God breathed life into Adam and they bonded together—Divine and human.

If the first sense created was smell, then it can also help us to read poetry effectively. A poem has an aroma— the paper on which it is printed, the book you found it in. Is it new, or as Emily says, "an antique volume"? Inhale it like air. Just as you would breathe in a good wine before raising it to your lips, breathe the poem before you read it. Words have an amazing power to stir the imagination and arouse the senses. Certain images conjure aromas: flowers, earth, sea, and snow, etc. Are the aromas harsh? Are they upsetting? A smell restores us to the origin of things. Scents often recall past memories. Do any words resonate with an event from your childhood or your adolescence? Familiar fragrances fly us back over time and space. The past can become present in an instant.

Inhale a poem deeply. Let God breathe new life into your heart through the words of a poem—as with the cycle of life, empty and full, the breath of a poem fills and empties.

4. OPEN YOUR HANDS!

Let go of whatever is burdening you when you read a poem. Unclench your hands; open your palms. Focus your complete attention on what you are reading. Touch the words on the page. They are the link between you and the poet. He or she labored to find the most meaningful words and to put them in their order and place. Reading poetry is tactile as well as visual and auditory. Hold the poem and turn the page. The poet invites you to touch certain emotions in your heart, to embrace your feelings. Imagine: what might this poem feel like if you could not see it on the page? If it were embodied?

When we open ourselves to God, we are more likely to receive divine guidance. It may not come immediately, but it will at some point, either as an inspiration or an intuition from deep within.

5. OPEN YOUR MOUTH!

Talk to yourself about what you have read. Talk about it with a friend. Discuss a poem with your spiritual director. Talk about it with God. Share your ideas with others. Remember that you are not being evaluated for your interpretation; this is not school—it is life! Reading a poem can be a joyful celebration. It can also be sad and depressing, but that can be helpful as well. A poem stirs many emotions, leads you in new directions, and helps you see what you may have missed or neglected before. Ask questions of those who might help you, someone who is already open to poetry's spirit. When you have spoken enough, be silent.

Remind yourself often why you pray.

6. OPEN YOUR HEART!

Above all, open your heart. A poem meant for you should make your heart beat faster. The poet opened his or her heart to you; now it is your turn to be open. There is conflict in every poem as there is in life; what about this poem…is its conflict yours? That of someone you know and love? Does the poem offer an answer to your own particular struggle? To theirs? In the film *Dead Poets Society*, Robin Williams tries to open his students' hearts to poetry, but discovers how difficult this is. When we only interpret a poem, we keep it at arm's length rather than embrace it. A specimen in a test tube is analyzed; a poem is *experienced*.

Let the poem *be* what it is. Most of all, does the poem take the top of your head off?

Suggested Poems for Prayer

The following represents a list of poems for further reading. In addition to my suggestions, I have included the recommendations of several of my friends and colleagues. It may be helpful for you to see why they recommend them and why a poem has special significance.

Coleridge, Samuel Taylor

> *Self-Knowledge* because it reminds me to put myself aside and direct everything I do toward a deeper knowledge of God.

Saint Augustine

> *The Beauty of Creation Bears Witness to God* because I know that God is close to me; I need only to look out of my window to see God's presence manifested.

Thompson, Francis

> *The Hound of Heaven* because so much spiritual beauty rises up from the gutter.

Peguy, Charles

> *God Speaks* because the poet makes God so reachable, touchable, loving, playful, and humorous.

Benson, Robert Hugh

> *After a Retreat* because I need to hear the simple message that God is love.

Powers, Jessica

> *The Garments of God* because I learn of God's compassion and forgiveness.

> *The House at Rest* because it gives me great insight into human nature.

Kilmer, Joyce

> *Trees* because I am that tree.

Herbert, George

> *The Call* because God's love is everlasting.

Frost, Robert

The Road Not Taken because I have learned to discern in the midst of nature.

Cummings, E. E.

We can't be born enough because physical birth and spiritual birth are "supremely welcome mysteries."

Donne, John

Holy Sonnet V because it calls me to conversion and discipleship.

Batter my heart because I so want to be conquered by God's love, but choose to lock God out instead.

Hymn to God my God, in my sicknesse because even in physical, spiritual, and emotional suffering, there is meaning.

Updike, John

Fever because it teaches me the reality of fragile health, death, and new life.

Seven Stanzas at Easter because it stresses the concrete reality of the resurrection.

Whitman, Walt

When I Heard the Learned Astronomer because it invites me to stillness, wordless praise, and awe at God's creation.

Plunkett, Joseph Mary

I See His Blood Upon the Rose because it is an invitation to love, seeing all creation as God's love letter, transparent with divine presence, in the passion of Jesus.

Oliver, Mary

The Summer Day because it teaches the importance of paying attention as the basis of prayer.

In Blackwater Woods because it teaches me the dance of loving and letting go.

Graves, Robert

The Cool Web because it teaches the importance of moving beyond language to ecstasy.

Rilke, Rainer Marie

> *The Arisen* because it invites me to persevere in my
> relationship with Jesus.

Kinnell, Gilway

> *Saint Francis and the Sow* because it speaks of
> relearning my blessedness through prayer.

OTHER POEMS:
Raleigh, Sir Walter

> *Passionate Man's Pilgrimage*

Milton, John

> *On the Morning of Christ's Nativity*

Herbert, George

> *Easter Wings*
> *Aaron*

Crashaw, Richard

> *Hymn to Saint Teresa*

Hopkins, Gerard Manley

> *The Wreck of the Deutschland*
>
> *Pied Beauty*
>
> *The Windhover: To Christ Our Lord*
>
> *Thou art indeed just Lord*
>
> *God's Grandeur*

Blake, William

> *Divine Image*
>
> *Holy Thursday*

Meredith, George

> *Lucifer in Starlight*

Savanarola, Girolamo

> *May I Love You, Lord*

Notes

Citations noted LED are from *The Life of Emily Dickinson*, by Richard B. Sewall. Harvard University Press, 1980.

Introduction

1. "The Gentian weaves her fringes—."
2. "Tell all the truth but tell it slant."
3. *The Prelude*, Bk. IV, ll. 334–337.
4. "I Dwell in Possibility."
5. June 1869, LED 460.
6. "The Poets light but lamps."
7. "This was a Poet."
8. Spring 1861, LED 481–482.
9. Spring 1861, LED 482.
10. "This is my letter to the world."

Chapter 1
A Brief Life of Miss Emily Dickinson

1. The original furniture and artifacts are preserved at Harvard University.
2. A second photograph may have been discovered. In May 2000, an English professor at the University of North Carolina, Chapel Hill, bought the photograph on an Internet auction website. In the photograph, she is older, perhaps in her early thirties, at the height of her creativity when she probably wrote a poem a day.
3. July 1862, LED 556.
4. LED 330.
5. Letter to Thomas Higginson, April 25, 1862, LED 57.
6. Letter of 1874, LED 74.
7. Conversation with Higginson, 1870.
8. April 5, 1862, LED 542.
9. "'Faith' is a fine invention."
10. June 7, 1862, LED 555.

11. Lyon divided the student body into three groups: "Christians," those who had accepted Christ; "Hopers," those who expressed the hope of accepting Christ; and "No-Hopers," of which Emily was one.

12. *My Personal Acquaintance with Emily Dickinson,* by Clara Newman Turner, family friend, as quoted in LED 360.

13. "Elysium is as far to go."

14. Letter home from Mt. Holyoke, 1848, LED 361.

15. Letter to a schoolmate at Mt. Holyoke, 1848, LED 364.

16. Like the English romantic poets and the American Transcendentalists, Emily advocated a natural piety. Although she never denied that God could speak through the medium of a clergyman, she listened for God to speak directly to her through her experience of external and human nature, and in her private prayer: "God preaches, a noted Clergyman— /," she notes, "And the sermon is never long."

17. "Some keep the Sabbath going to Church—."

18. A photograph of the Irish servants hangs in the Dickinson home.

19. February 1863, LED 561.

20. Letter to Mr. and Mrs. Holland, 1858, LED 604.

21. September 1859, LED 603.

22. February 1863, LED 561.

23. January 13, 1854, LED 401.

24. "My life closed twice before its close."

25. Letter to Mr. and Mrs. Holland, November 1858, LED 604.

26. "I'm Nobody! Who are you?"

27. "Publication—is the Auction."

28. June 1864, LED 636. Emily wove her poems into little hand bound books she called *fascicles* around 1858, and stopped producing them around 1864. In the end, there were about forty which, upon her death, were dismembered and published in many different ways.

29. "The Soul that hath a Guest."

30. In a letter to Mabel Loomis Todd, American author and friend, Emily wrote: "She wore white, she shut herself away from her race as a mark of her separation from the mass of minds."

31. Lavinia broke a promise to Emily to burn the poems, but instead destroyed only the letters.

32. Austin's diary entry, May 15, 1886, LED 125.

33. *The Springfield Republican*, May 19, 1886 (written by Susan Dickinson, Emily's sister-in-law).

34. "Ample make this Bed—."

35. Todd edited and deciphered much of Emily's material in the first edition of the poems along with Higginson. Emily's poems were edited because, as Higginson said, they displayed "rough rhythms and imperfect rhymes," incorrect spelling and poor grammar.

Chapter 2
Emily's Poetry as Prayer

1. "At least to pray is left."

2. "Prayer is the little implement."

3. "The Matryr Poets—did not tell—."

4. "'Secrets' is a daily word."

5. "To a Young Contributor," in *The New Atlantic Monthly*.

6. "Essential oils are wrung."

7. "Prayer is the little implement."

8. "The Martyr Poets—did not tell—."

Chapter 3
Emily and God

1. In chapter 167 of her *Dialogues*, we read: "Eternal God, eternal Trinity,…You are a mystery as deep as the sea; the more I search, the more I find, and the more I find, the more I search for you."

2. "Aurora Leigh."

3. October 25, 1851, LED 59.

4. A four-wheeled horse-drawn vehicle.

5. Letter to Mrs. Henry Hills, 1884, LED 590.

Chapter 4
Emily and Nature

1. April 25, 1862, LED 542.

2. cf. "Tell all the truth but tell it slant—."

3. October 1883, LED 204.

4. Emily knew the passage in the New Testament where Christ praises the Father for hiding the mysteries of the kingdom from the wise and the clever and revealing them to children (cf. Mt 11:25).

5. "To My Sister."

6. 1861, LED 482.

Chapter 5
Emily and Prayer

1. Martin Buber, *I and Thou* (1923).

2. Letter to Helen Jackson, 1884, LED 590.

3. August 1862, LED 590.

4. Autumn, 1853, LED 597.

5. August 1862, LED 590.

Chapter 6
Emily's Faith and Doubt

1. November 1882, LED 640.

2. *Hamlet*, iii.

3. When Emily was in her forties, LED 201.

Chapter 7
Emily and Death

1. October 1851, LED 435.

2. April 25, 1862, LED 542.

3. Letter to her cousin, John Graves, April, 1856, LED 406.

4. "There's been a Death, in the Opposite House."

5. November 1858, LED 604.

6. April 1856, LED 406.

7. *Macbeth*, IV.

8. Letter to Thomas Higginson, Spring 1876, LED 403.

9. January 1863, LED 632.

10. 1877, LED 563.

11. April 15, 1862, LED 541.

12. April 25, 1862, LED 542.

Reverend John Delli Carpini, Ph.D. is the author of *Prayer and Piety in the Poems of Gerard Manley Hopkins* and writes often on spirituality and literature.

BOOKS & MEDIA

The Daughters of St. Paul operate book and media centers at the following addresses. Visit, call or write the one nearest you today, or find us on the World Wide Web, www.pauline.org

CALIFORNIA
3908 Sepulveda Blvd, Culver City, CA
   90230   310-397-8676
5945 Balboa Avenue, San Diego, CA
   92111   858-565-9181
46 Geary Street, San Francisco, CA
   94108   415-781-5180

FLORIDA
145 S.W. 107th Avenue, Miami, FL
   33174   305-559-6715

HAWAII
1143 Bishop Street, Honolulu, HI
   96813   808-521-2731
Neighbor Islands call: 800-259-8463

ILLINOIS
172 North Michigan Avenue,
   Chicago, IL 60601   312-346-4228

LOUISIANA
4403 Veterans Blvd, Metairie, LA
   70006   504-887-7631

MASSACHUSETTS
Rte. 1, 885 Providence Hwy,
   Dedham, MA 02026
   781-326-5385

MISSOURI
9804 Watson Road, St. Louis, MO
   63126   314-965-3512

NEW JERSEY
561 U.S. Route 1, Wick Plaza,
   Edison, NJ 08817
   732-572-1200

NEW YORK
150 East 52nd Street, New York, NY
   10022   212-754-1110
78 Fort Place, Staten Island, NY
   10301   718-447-5071

OHIO
2105 Ontario Street, Cleveland, OH
   44115   216-621-9427

PENNSYLVANIA
9171-A Roosevelt Blvd, Philadelphia,
   PA 19114   215-676-9494

SOUTH CAROLINA
243 King Street, Charleston, SC
   29401   843-577-0175

TENNESSEE
4811 Poplar Avenue, Memphis, TN
   38117   901-761-2987

TEXAS
114 Main Plaza, San Antonio, TX
   78205   210-224-8101

VIRGINIA
1025 King Street, Alexandria, VA
   22314   703-549-3806

CANADA
3022 Dufferin Street, Toronto, Ontario,
   Canada M6B 3T5
   416-781-9131
1155 Yonge Street, Toronto, Ontario,
   Canada M4T 1W2
   416-934-3440

¡También somos su fuente para libros, videos y música en español!